Every Writer's Dream:
The Insider's Path to an
Indie Bestseller

BOOKS BY MARC ALAN EDELHEIT

Chronicles of a Legionary Officer:
Book One: **Stiger's Tigers**
Book Two: **The Tiger**
Book Three: **The Tiger's Fate**
Book Four: **The Tiger's Time**
Book Five: **The Tiger's Wrath** (Coming 2019)

Tales of the Seventh:
Part One: **Stiger**
Part Two: **Fort Covenant**
Part Three: **A Dark Foretoken**
Part Four: **Thresh (Coming 2020)**

The Karus Saga:
Book One: **Lost Legio IX**
Book Two: **Fortress of Radiance**
Book Three: **The First Compact** (Coming 2019)

Way of the Legend:
With Quincy J. Allen
Book One: **Reclaiming Honor** (Coming 2019)
Book Two: (Coming 2020)

Every Writer's Dream: The Insider's Path to an Indie Bestseller

Everything I wish I would've known before I self-published

Marc Alan Edelheit

Everything I Wish I Would've Known Before I Self-Published

First Edition

Copyright © 2019 by Marc Edelheit. All rights reserved, including the right to reproduce this book, or portions thereof, in any form. No part of this text may be reproduced, transmitted, downloaded, decompiled, reverse engineered, or stored in or introduced into any information storage and retrieval system, in any form or by any means, whether electronic or mechanical, without the express written permission of the author. The scanning, uploading, and distribution of this book via the Internet or via any other means without the permission of the publisher is illegal and punishable by law. Please purchase only authorized electronic editions and do not participate in or encourage electronic piracy of copyrighted materials.

This book is an informational resource for people seeking to self-publish and market a book. The information contained in this book is based on the personal experiences of Marc Edelheit and shared in the hopes that it will ignite you to create action in your life. Marc Edelheit is not a tax advisor or attorney. The information in this book should not be interpreted as professional advice.

The author of this book assumes no responsibility or liability for any consequences resulting directly or indirectly from any action or inaction you take based on the information found within or material linked to this book. The author of this book cannot guarantee the outcomes of following the general recommendations and statements about potential outcomes. The author of this book specifically disclaims any implied or expressed warranties about the information and recommendations provided herein.

I wish to thank my agent, Andrea Hurst, for her invaluable support and assistance. I would also like to thank my beta readers, who suffered through several early drafts. My betas: Paul Klebaur, Bruce Heaven, Tim Adams, Paul Bersoux, David Houston, Sheldon Levy, Michael Hetts, Bill Schnippert, Jimmy McAfee, Joel Raining, and William Grahm. I would also like to take a moment to thank my loving wife, who sacrificed many an evening and weekend to allow me to work on my writing.

Editing Assistance by Hannah Streetman, Audrey Mackaman, Brandon Purcell, and Special Editing and Layout Assistance by Elizabeth Edelheit.

Art by Piero Mng (Gianpiero Mangialardi)
Cover Design and Formatting by 100 Covers
Agented by Andrea Hurst & Associates
http://maenovels.com/

Contents

Introduction ·································· vii
    About the Author
    Introduction

Chapter One ···································· 1
    Writing Is a Business
    Business Planning

Chapter Two ··································· 13
    Marc's Writing Method in Steps
    Just Write

Chapter Three ································· 25
    The Editing Matters
    Different Types of Editing
    Being Open to Feedback
    Agents

Chapter Four ·································· 48
    To Self-Publish or Not
    Traditional Publishing vs. Indie
    The Advantages of Amazon & Kindle Unlimited

Chapter Five **60**
The Essentials Every Author Needs for Marketing Success

Chapter Six **77**
Book Marketing
Building a Successful Marketing Plan
Marketing Tools
Marketing Outlets
Sample Marketing Plans/Campaigns
Sample Templates: Book Budget, Marketing Budget, Marketing Campaign
Book Outline

Chapter Seven **117**
Important Lists: Most Everything an Author Needs to Build Their Brand & Sell Books
Audio Publishers, Self-Publishing/Distributors, Self-Publishing Services/Presses, Cover Designers, Editorial Services, Author Tools, eBook Design, Writing Support, Promotional Marketing Websites, Book Review Services, Author Website Developers, Book Awards, Author Website Developers, Industry Watchdog/ Professional Association Groups

Introduction

About the Author • Introduction

Bottom line: I can't guarantee you will be successful.

That's right. I cannot and will not guarantee you will become a successful author after reading this book. I simply do not have a crystal ball to look into the future to make this determination. Isn't that a switch from others who promise you will publish the next bestseller or make six figures after following their suggestions?

Self-publishing a book can be easy, but making it as a successful author is difficult. To be frank, and that's what I will be in this book, it is impossible for me to make you any guarantee of success. So, I just won't do it. What I will do, however, is share with you tips, secrets, and tricks of the trade that helped me reach the status of bestselling author so that you can skip through the struggles and have fewer frustrations along the way.

I will also provide lists of marketing sites, tools, and publishing services amongst other useful resources to give you the edge when it comes to competing for readers.

Warning: I do caution you to read everything and not to skim. This book is not full of fluff and all information contained in it has been critical to my success. Failure to do so may cause you to miss something vital, and that could cost you future sales.

Marc's Rule: Do your research!

Before you purchase other books like this one, I always *recommend* checking to see what other works the author has published. Make certain they walk the talk. If they promise to make you the next bestselling author... have they themselves had any success in the marketplace? Has their success been only with books to help others improve as an author or have they written a few fiction bestsellers?

If so, how many reviews do they have? Are there only a handful of reviews, overwhelmingly negative or mediocre? Do your research. It's important in this business to be sure you're getting advice from people who have achieved a high level of success. And there are more than a few out there who have written books to help you along the way.

Basically, you want to take suggestions from people who have been there and done that, authors who know what they are talking about.

What are my credentials? Well, as of writing this book, I have published nine novels in four years, ten books, if you include this one, and moved well over 300,000 eBooks while racking up over 60,000,000 Kindle Unlimited page reads. Yes, that is 60 million KU! I expect by the end of 2019 to have exceeded 100,000,000 Kindle Unlimited page reads. And these numbers do not include the thousands of print or audiobooks sold. I've accomplished all of this not only in just four years, but as a self-started independent writer.

I have also made the Kindle All-Star list, multiple times. Kindle All-Stars are those authors who are read the most in

Kindle Unlimited and the Kindle Owner's Lending Library on a given monthly basis. In addition, I have been lucky enough to win three Independent Publisher Book Awards.

My first book, *Stiger's Tigers*, won the bronze medal for Best Fantasy in 2016. My third novel, *The Tiger's Fate*, won gold in 2017. *The Tiger's Time* won bronze for Best Adult Fiction in 2019. One of my series, Chronicles of an Imperial Legionary Officer, was a 2019 finalist for Best Series in the Next Generation Indie Book Awards.

I've been one of those fortunate few who have done exceptionally well as a self-published author, and I believe in giving back by actively mentoring and providing consulting services to aspiring authors. I find that I continue to repeat myself often and that's why I decided to write this book, which is almost exclusively focused on self-publishing fiction on the Amazon platform and KDP Select.

It is not a plodding, painfully detailed treatise on how to write and market a novel. Instead, this book, which can be for the first-time or the seasoned author, is more of a high-level overview of what every author must do and have in place to increase the chances of being successful as an Indie author in the current marketplace.

I share what I've learned through trial and error as a self-published author. I intend on educating you so that you can make informed decisions about your own writing and publishing paths. It is my sincere hope that you see as much success as I have and, after reading this book, you come away having learned something valuable that helps make you the next bestselling author.

If I can do it, there is no reason why others can't realize success.

Chapter One

Writing Is a Business • Business Planning

Bottom Line: It's a business, dummy—not a hobby or a get-rich-quick scheme.

That's right. I'm going to give it to you straight. This is a business and you must approach it as such. Don't look at publishing your first or your sixth book as a hobby, because it's not.

Everyone you will be working with, from an agent (if you are lucky enough to snag one), to a small press, editors, illustrators, Amazon, etc., will view what you are doing as a business. It is their business to make money, and it should be yours, too. There is nothing wrong with making money. Embrace this mentality, especially if you want to become a full-time author.

Self-publishing a book is easy but making it as a successful author is difficult. Publishing is a cutthroat business. There are tens of thousands of other self-published authors out there, and you are directly competing with them for readers.

It's important you understand something right now, before we go further: Breakaway hits are the exception, not the rule. For the vast majority of you reading this book, it simply won't happen and, worse, may never happen, no matter how many books you publish.

In this market, to become successful, it takes hard work and a lot of effort. Let me repeat myself. It takes hard work and *a lot* of effort to be successful. Heck, anything done right is hard work. If you're going to put the time into writing a book, you might as well do everything possible to help increase the chances of having some success. That is why it is important to create a business and marketing plan. Without one, your chances of growing your brand decrease dramatically.

What is your brand?
It's how you identify and share your story as an author. What you share on social media, the style of books you write, the professionalism, enthusiasm, emotions, and quirkiness you inject into your work. The way you develop your persona, package it, and present it to the world, that is your brand. You want to stand out from the crowd and create authority. Like it or not, you are or will soon become an influencer. It is important to note that when I speak on brand it is not in relation to branding a book or series. That is a different topic for a future book.

The greater your reach, the more readers you will impact and therefore the more successful you will become with each successive launch. Why is that? When your book climbs higher in the ranks, it becomes visible to more prospective readers, who might be open to giving you a chance. The more impactful your brand becomes, the greater your author platform and the more sought after you will become.

What is your author platform?
How visible you, as an author, are to your target audience, meaning how well you stand out from the pack. Publishers rely upon this when making decisions as to whether or not to buy a book from a given author. You don't need to have a

platform to get picked up, but it helps, and it all starts with building your brand.

Marc's Rule: Make a business plan.

Remember, this is a business, and a successful business has a plan. To achieve success as an author, you need a business plan. When I self-published my first book, there was no one waiting to give me any *real or useful* advice. Sure, I read articles online and even picked up a few books on how to self-publish. When it came time to launch my book, I felt educated, like I knew what I was doing.

In hindsight, much of what I thought I had learned was rubbish and next to useless. The majority of the advice I received was worthless, misleading, or just plain wrong. I discovered that there are plenty of people out there giving advice, but few who give good advice. As a result, I made mistakes.

In truth, I am a little hard on myself. My family tells me this all the time. I think most authors are their worst critics and regularly beat themselves up. It's just who we are and built into our creative DNA. We think that to be an artist is to suffer, but you don't have to do this alone. This book is going to help you with useful tips and resources.

Part of living is learning, and to gain experience, you will make mistakes. I did a lot right with my first book, *Stiger's Tigers*, while at the same time, some of the things I did were wrong. I learned, adjusted, and worked to keep from making those same mistakes again. Once I developed a business plan, I found that it helped me tremendously in minimizing mistakes and keeping me focused on my new business, being an author. As a result, I've slowly but surely seen tremendous growth in my brand and author platform, but things did not happen overnight.

Authors are entrepreneurs and writing is their business.

Understand that, before we move on, this is a business book, and nothing is more integral to your success as a writer than firmly setting this concept in your mind. The next step is to come up with a detailed plan on how to approach the marketplace. This involves sitting down and developing a business strategy, budget, and marketing plan.

Most of you reading this book are likely already authors or you've always wanted to be one. Maybe you're prepping to launch your first book or perhaps you finally decided to get serious about writing a novel. For me, it was a single moment of inspiration that did it. I got serious and, almost by accident, it turned into my full-time job.

Back in 2014, I was driving to the Jersey shore with my family to spend a long weekend with my parents. I was looking forward to relaxing at the beach and playing with my kids on the boardwalk. Well, we were stuck in traffic on the Atlantic City Expressway. It was around seven in the morning and there's nothing I hate more than traffic. The highway looked like a parking lot and cars were not moving. The coffee was strong, and my mental wheels were turning. Oh, did I mention I hate traffic? I utterly loathe it with a passion.

Everyone else in the car was asleep. At the time, I had both a successful history podcast and a corporate career. While I sat miserably in traffic, stewing in frustration at the lack of progress towards our destination, I began thinking about my next podcast episode and the research it would entail. My mind began to wander to a book I had been trying to write for some time. Then, it suddenly hit me…the same amount of effort I was putting into the podcast could go into writing a book.

I'd always wanted to write a novel. I had a ton of great ideas. I repeatedly started to write and stopped and then started again. Why could I never finish? The thought nagged at me as I sat in traffic. I was a doer, a go-getter. In business, when something needed doing, I attacked it head on and got it done. So, what was keeping me from finishing a book?

The lanes to my right and left began to move, while mine didn't budge. The answer became glaringly obvious. Nothing was keeping me from writing a book—but me. I was the hindrance. I decided then and there to stop making excuses. I would put my podcast on hold, set aside the time required to write, and finish my first book, even if it killed me.

That was the moment of magic, an epiphany sent from Minerva herself. As incredible as it now seems, lightning struck as I was sitting, frustrated beyond belief, in traffic on the Atlantic City Expressway. The Universe spoke and my life has never been the same since.

So then, the next question was, what do I write about? Even though I was a successful executive, there was no thought given to a business plan. I approached my first book as an artistic piece of work and gave no consideration for an overall business strategy. I had resolved to write a book, and by gum, I'd do it.

I was not thinking of my writing as a business, at least not yet. In that moment of decision, I did something right, while at the same time I got something else fundamentally wrong. Can you guess what it was? Yep, that's right, not thinking of my writing as a business.

When my first book launched, it sold incredibly well without any marketing or outreach, and there was no business plan in place to support my venture. Even though I made a good-sized splash, it could have been so much bigger had I known then what I know now.

Marc's Rule: Plan ahead; think strategically.

Don't make the same mistake I did. Plan ahead. Think strategically and develop a business plan to assist you with the process of making a larger splash. The more organized and prepared you are for your launch, the more you will grow your platform and the closer you will come to making writing your full-time profession.

To get there, you must understand what a business plan is and how to use one. A business plan is simply a document that outlines your goals, then details how to achieve them. Sounds simple, right? For those who never worked with a business plan, it can also sound scary, perhaps even daunting. But it shouldn't be.

There are many variations and innumerable ideas on what should comprise a business plan. You can hit Google, poke around, and learn more about them if you wish. I recommend you do. The more educated and knowledgeable you are, the better.

There are entire courses taught on how to properly develop and implement a business plan. Okay...stop hyperventilating. Don't panic; don't stress. Your plan doesn't have to be anything fancy. In truth, there is no one set way to build or make it. A plan is simply that—a plan of action, a blueprint for you to follow as you go through the process of launching your first, fifth, or one hundredth book.

Your plan can be written down on a pad of paper or typed up into a document. It is up to you. The important concept to get here is that the plan is going to lay out what you are going to do to try to make your splash in the publishing pool larger and grander. Try not to overthink this. You don't need an MBA to draft a business plan.

What are the fundamentals of a business plan?

These are my basics and I boil them down into six points:

1. **SET GOALS**: Come up with an objective and an overall plan on how to achieve it. Define what you want to do. Then write a plan for making it happen. Essentially you will be designing a business strategy on how you are going to execute. This often will require a trial-and-error approach.

Prior to becoming a full-time author, I was a businessman. When we launched a new product, we came up with a business plan. Guess what? Several of the initial plans we came up with were wrong or flawed in some way. Did we give up? Nope. To quote *Galaxy Quest*, "Never give up, never surrender." We reviewed the data, analyzed what we had learned, made changes, and rolled with the punches, often succeeding beyond our wildest imaginings.

When it comes to publishing, it is important to continually analyze and review the data related to your plan and adjust accordingly, such as changing your marketing strategy if needed. This is a must if you want to become a successful author.

2. **DETERMINE YOUR IDEAL CUSTOMER**: Identify and focus on your customers. Those are your readers. They are the end users of your product and the ones you hope will fall in love with your work and continue to purchase your books for years to come. Figure out who they are and write not only for yourself, but for them. All your marketing efforts will go towards exposing your books to similar people and converting prospective readers into sales.

If you understand your target market segment and what your customers want, you're ahead of the curve. You will be in a good position to start building your author platform. That, in a nutshell, is the game. If you grow, you win. If you don't, you lose.

3. **DEVELOP A BUDGET**: This is a business; there is cash flow. At the beginning of the process, before publication, all the cash will be flowing out. Examples of outflow expenses are cover design, editorial assistance, manuscript formatting, and website development, just to name a few.

Keep track of what you spend, because these are all business expenses. If you don't understand how tax deductions work, contact a tax advisor. In fact, I fully recommend you do. Get some professional advice. Listen to people who know what they're talking about. Don't rely on Google or Wikipedia for your answers. You're just asking for trouble and creating future problems for yourself if you don't work with an experienced professional.

Most tax advisors, or Certified Public Accountants (CPA), offer a free consultation. If they don't, they are not the kind of people you want to work with. Speak with several to determine which one will be the best fit and the most helpful, responsive, and knowledgeable about the kind of work you are doing. The objective here is for you to pick a professional to help your business remain financially healthy and in accordance with tax law.

A rule of thumb for publishing your own work is to use *professionals*. This is especially important in launching your first book. All it takes is a few mistakes and you can not only damage your brand but irreparably harm it. If your book's formatting is messed up, text is riddled with typos and the plot has holes large enough to drive a car through, it's locked in landscape mode, or a hundred other issues pop up, you may see a slew of negative reviews. If that happens, you've just dug yourself a hole from which you may not be able to pull yourself out.

Marc's Rule: Hire professionals.

Until you absolutely know what you are doing, get a professional to do the publishing part for you. The peace of mind alone is worth it.

In relation to the outflow of cash, begin budgeting. Start setting aside the funds you will need long before you complete your book. Create a marketing war chest. Your novel will be competing against thousands of other books for the attention of readers. You will need several thousand dollars for this process.

It's better to put this money aside in advance, rather than waiting till the last moment. Open a savings account and deposit a little bit of each paycheck to help you grow an operational funds account. It's better to have the monies readily available when you need them than to go into debt just to publish your first book.

The burden of revolving debt with high interest rates can be very stressful. Increasing your debt to publish a book makes it more difficult for you to get your next book out. This is especially true if your first book doesn't make a splash. Additional debt is just not worth it.

4. **CREATE A MARKETING CAMPAIGN**: This is a business; marketing is required. Translation: shamelessly promote yourself. Marketing is required if you are going to self-publish. Don't kid yourself into believing you won't need to spread the word about your book. Its awesomeness alone most likely won't spread by word of mouth. You will need help, and that's where marketing comes in.

If you want to make a splash, you will need to conduct a marketing campaign. Without marketing, your splash in the publishing pool will be a ripple.

With each book launch, I use a wide variety of marketing techniques to achieve a desired splash, such as book marketing sites, advertising, press releases, etc.

5. **REVIEW ANALYTICS**: Analyze any and all data. Self-publishing, along with online marketing services, comes with a ton of great metrics for you to study and deconstruct. I know the thought of having to analyze metrics sounds scary and not something you want to do...but honestly, learning how to read marketing data is not terribly hard. It is what you infer from it that matters. Make the effort to understand the reporting that is provided to you. The more you know about your target audience—the readers who are currently buying your books or the new readers you want to reach—the more effective you will be at getting the word out for future releases.

You can easily search Google or YouTube for tutorials on how to use certain marketing sites, like Amazon Marketing Services or Google Ads. There are also plenty of tutorials that explain how to look at their reports to maximize your marketing dollars. There is no excuse for not learning. It is bad business to not even try because your success depends on it.

6. **REFINE YOUR APPROACH**: Your business plan is never finished. It's true. Refine, adjust, analyze, and improve your business plan continually. It seems like there are new marketing techniques and services emerging every day. Be on the lookout for new opportunities.

I just added a product merchandising line, where my readers can go to my website to purchase themed shirts, hats, mugs, and bags. Cool, right?

Not only is it totally awesome for the fan, but now my readers are walking around in themed gear and acting as passive marketing. This is a perfect example of revisiting a business plan to fit my target audience's needs. Keep in mind business plans may change in ways you never anticipate. If you get a deal/offer from a traditional publisher, you will need to change your plan accordingly. Just because you snag a publishing deal does not mean you will be wildly successful. Brand building is still required.

Sample Product Merchandise:

RECAP: Writing and self-publishing is a business. There is nothing to debate on this point. To run a business, you need a plan.

Your business plan should include:

1. Setting goals/objectives & strategy to achieve
2. Determining your ideal customer
3. Developing a budget
4. Creating a marketing campaign
5. Reviewing and analyzing all data
6. Refining your approach

Once you have developed a solid business plan and begin to follow it, you will increase the chances of achieving success and making a larger splash in the publishing pool.

Chapter Two

Marc's Writing Method in Steps • Just Write

Bottom Line: So, you want to write a book, eh? Are you mad?

I approach my writing in a precise and detailed manner. It works for me, and very well, too. I've written and published nine books in four years. During three of those years, I had a full-time job. All of my books, in their genre, have been #1 Amazon bestsellers. That said, I am certain my approach will not be a good fit for everyone, but creating a plan is one of the most important steps to remaining motivated throughout the process.

One of the great things about writing is that there is no one set way to go about writing the next great novel. If your style of writing works better for you, awesome. If not, that's why I'm sharing my method, so that you might try it. Whatever works, use that. The focus should be on getting the job done, and in the end that's all that matters. The best business plan in the world won't help you become a full-time author if you can't finish a book.

My Method in Steps

STEP ONE: The idea. You need a fresh and exciting idea that will capture the prospective reader's imagination.

Remember, you are writing to entertain. Not only are you an artist, a smith of words, but also an entertainer. Embrace it. Write for your target audience—those are the readers you identified in your business plan. They are the ones who matter when it comes to building your author platform.

Marc's Rule: Keep it simple, stupid.

Not only do you want to write for your planned audience, but my personal advice is to keep your first book simple from a structural standpoint. What do I mean by that? Until you establish yourself as an author with a good-sized following, focus on writing stories that are straightforward. Tell your stories from one point of view. Head-hopping should be avoided. Readers can find it annoying and confusing if not done correctly. I made this mistake, not even realizing it was a problem in my first book. And guess what? It cost me reviews.

A good developmental editor will help you avoid head-hopping and other basic mistakes. If you don't know what head hopping is, look it up on Google. It's probably not a bad idea for you to familiarize yourself with different perspectives (first person, third person limited vs. omniscient, etc.) to help keep point of view consistent.

At the same time, make sure you listen to your editor. Google and Wikipedia are certainly not substitutes for a good editor's advice. Note: There are times when using such platforms are completely acceptable and other times when professionals should be consulted.

Ever heard the acronym KISS? The military likes to use it and so do I. Keep it simple, stupid. The more complicated your story, the more difficult it will be to write.

Over the years, I have spoken with a good number of aspiring writers struggling to finish their first book. More often than not they struggle because their story is far too complex from a structural standpoint. With my many attempts at writing a book, I know for a fact I suffered from the curse of plot complexity. It was one of the factors keeping me from finishing a novel. When I finally got serious about writing, I made sure *Stiger's Tigers* was a simple, straightforward story. That alone made writing my first published book much easier and not an exercise in frustration.

If you are looking to push yourself technically as a writer, the place to do that is not with your first book. Once you've published your debut novel, and only at that point, would I recommend looking to challenge yourself as a writer, and then gradually so. In fact, I would encourage it. I try to push myself with each subsequent release, upping my game. I like to think I've been successful at doing this. However, as I've said, I would advise caution on that with your first and maybe even your second novel. Remember KISS.

STEP TWO: The outline. A lot of people hate outlines. Know that I am also one of them. I learned that loathing in school, because my teachers could not effectively show me how outlining would be a benefit to me.

It's kind of like algebra. I could never see how I could possibly use it in life. Truth be told, I've not used algebra since college, and what I did in my math class might not be called algebra. I'm terrible at math and even needed remedial help. It's a good thing my strengths lie in writing and not engineering. I saw a tee shirt the other day that said, *another day has passed and I'm still not using algebra*. I almost bought it.

I have come to value and rely upon outlines, and unlike algebra, I use them often.

Outlines are, in my mind, critically important to writing a solid book. It's not just all about writing. Understand it takes more to make a book good than just putting in daily word counts. I can't tell you how many aspiring and struggling authors I hear proudly proclaiming they wrote four thousand words in a given day, or five thousand the next. That's all fine and dandy, but the quality of the output is what matters.

Outlines help give thought, substance, and structure to your writing. They provide you a chance to roadmap the story and character arcs. You get to look at everything critically, raising the stakes whenever possible. If you're not using an outline, why not? Don't fall into the trap of thinking that daily word counts are all that matter. Writing a bestseller is about so much more, and pulling it off successfully, in my opinion, requires planning. Always plan for success.

"How do you handle writer's block?" I get asked this a lot, and I mean *a lot*. I bump into aspiring writers all the time who complain about writer's block. It is a serious issue.

"I don't suffer from writer's block," I say, "ever."

That answer seems to surprise. It's the truth, because I use an outline. When I question these hopeful writers, who are looking to me for a nugget of wisdom, I find they invariably have the same problem. No outline, no real plan.

I've found through personal experience, if you have a chapter-by-chapter outline, essentially a blueprint for your book, the writing goes more smoothly. You know what you have to write before you begin the writing. There is no thinking it up organically as you sit down at your desk, kitchen table, or coffee shop.

In my humble opinion, outlines make writing a novel manageable. I know this for a fact, because I wrote *Stiger, Tales of the Seventh Part One* organically and without an outline. I wanted to see the difference between preplanning and making it up as I went.

Could I still deliver a quality book? I wasn't sure, but I was willing to try. The end result: It was more challenging for me to pull off a really good book, which I managed to still do. It also took longer to write and added to my stress levels. On the bright side, that book currently has 485 reviews on Amazon, with a 4.8 average rating. So, to use an outline or not? Both paths work. It really boils down to what works best for you. My recommendation is to use an outline. I found it more difficult without one.

"So, Marc, tell us about your outlining process." Okay, well, I thought you'd never ask. An outline doesn't have to be terribly detailed. Mine aren't, at least in the beginning. It can start out simple and written out with a pen on a pad. Don't overthink this. At the minimum, all your outline must do is create that basic blueprint for you to follow. That's it. You choose how detailed you want it to be. My outlines start out very simple, and over time I work on them, adding depth to the point where they become surprisingly complex, providing an excellent roadmap.

For each chapter, I begin with the characters in the scene, time of day, weather, setting, the objective I wish to accomplish, and a brief summary. That's it. As I map out my story through my outline, I take about a month to work on it. Sometimes, two months are required. It all depends upon the size of the book and the number of chapters. Every day, I spend an hour or two adding to it, refining the plot, working on specific chapters or on character arcs...striving to tie everything together and to increase the stakes wherever possible.

Basically, I pick at the outline a little each day, adding the detail and depth, until I am satisfied that it's a good blueprint and has everything I need to begin writing. I don't ever share my ideas with anyone, not even my wife. The first person who sees my manuscript is my developmental editor, and only after the book is written.

I have very strong opinions about this, as I don't want anyone to contaminate my creative process. Contaminate the creative process? What the hell are you talking about? How can someone do that?

Have you ever asked a friend their thoughts on the story you are working on? Told someone an idea you had? Did they give you blunt feedback you were not expecting or offer some unhelpful suggestions? I've been there.

Simply put, my experience has been that when you solicit advice, typically you get feedback you don't need to hear. It's why I no longer share or ask. In social situations, when questioned about what I'm working on, my answer is, "No spoilers." Or, "Something cool." Then I make a point of changing the subject. "Nice weather we've been having."

Sure, there are some people out there worth soliciting advice from, but honestly…there are very few I would even consider.

Generally, when you get feedback from a friend, their half-nanosecond of thought about plot or characters can easily corrupt and damage your vision. You're the one who's been thinking on this story for weeks, months, or even years. It is precisely this kind of half-baked feedback that can put doubts in your head. It can easily see you questioning your entire concept. This can and, in my experience, will hurt your writing in ways you can't begin to imagine. So, I avoid it at all cost.

Marc's Rule: If you think your idea for a book is cool, run with it.

Don't listen to naysayers and don't solicit feedback.

Chances are, your idea is very cool. You came up with it, nurtured it, and then gave birth to it – through the writing process – in the form of a book. Be careful of letting others pollute your concept. Disregard me at your peril. Heck, it's your story. In the end you will do what you want anyway. I can only offer my advice, and I've always found the process worked better for me when I did not tell a soul about what I was working on.

STEP THREE: Once I have my outline set, I write my book from beginning to end. Don't stress about your story being perfect as you put pen to paper or finger to key. Just write the damn thing and let it come out. Think of this process like an exorcism. Let the demons out, or in this case, let the words out.

For years, I made the mistake of trying to edit as I wrote. I would write a chapter and then try to edit that chapter. It was a frustrating process for me, because I could never, ever get each chapter quite perfect. The end result was always the same. I couldn't go the distance and finish.

When I finally decided to get serious, it dawned on me to try writing the book from beginning to end…without doing any editing or making improvements until the book was completed.

Why is this important?
Because I found that by writing and not stopping to edit, the process keeps moving forward. The creative juices, uninhibited by frustration derived from editing, continue flowing. In addition, it takes the pressure off for making

things immediately perfect. You get to put that headache off till later in the process. Once my manuscript was complete, I could return to it with fresh eyes and ideas to fill in the depth, shadows, and accents just like a work of art.

Writing followed immediately by editing made the project frustrating. I could never quite perfect my work to my liking. Day after day I would toil away on a given chapter. I found myself plodding along until it became downright depressing. I would get to the point where I did not seem to be making much progress. Worse, when I finally managed to finish a chapter, the next one loomed, just waiting for the same treatment.

It became frustration incarnate. The joy of writing a book slowly began to be leeched out of the project that had at one time sparked intense excitement. Eventually and almost inevitably, that book I was struggling with would become yet another failed project that I pushed aside for a later time. Working this way makes the climb up that proverbial mountain seem much steeper.

For me, the actual creative part of writing is always the most enjoyable part. Crafting something from nothing is fun. The improvement phase or editing phase is where you get down and dirty, digging in between the lines of text. This part is not so much fun. In my opinion, editing is pure work and a terrible grind. If you write and then immediately edit every chapter, you know you're going to continue to have to repeat the process over and over again.

Writing this way became work. I found myself looking for other things to do, like straightening up my office or sharpening those pencils I've not used in ten years.

So, after some reflection, the natural thing to do was to separate the two processes.

Writers just want to write and have the words flow out perfectly. The problem is, they never come out exactly how you want them to on the first try. Not even if you're Thomas Jefferson. Have you ever sat down to read the Declaration of Independence? I wish I could write as fine as that man. In truth, even Thomas Jefferson had to go through numerous drafts on the Declaration of Independence.

So, for me, writing the story from beginning to end makes sense. I don't edit. I will not work to improve what I've written until I have a complete product. Once you have a manuscript completely written, your first draft, it's much easier to finish the book because the entire story is already there. All you must now do is slog away at each chapter, working to take it to the next level.

Hey, Marc, isn't that the very thing you were trying to avoid when you separated the writing from the editing?

Well, not quite.

As I've said, writing a novel is like climbing a mountain. Looking up, the mountain appears quite tall. If it's over 3,000 feet from base to summit, unless you're an experienced mountaineer, you might find yourself wondering if you can even do it.

I discovered that, by having a complete product, the story written from beginning to end, editing seemed like a more manageable process. I found myself looking at my book in a different way once it was written out in a first draft form. Okay, I say to myself, there are eighteen chapters, plus an epilogue, to improve. The slog to the epilogue will be difficult, grueling, and at times quite painful, but guess what? The end is in sight and the book is already written. I just have to keep working towards that epilogue.

Every time I start a new book, I feel like that inexperienced person at the base of the mountain, looking up. However, because I've done it, I know that the processes I've developed work for me and there is nothing to worry about. At some point, I will reach the summit. So, too, can you.

Trust me on this: To be a writer is to perpetually be frustrated. Your work, no matter how good it actually is, will never be good enough for you. That's just how things are. Accept that truth now. If you do, you will be a more effective writer. And if you feel your work is perfect as is, with no room for improvement, I feel very confident telling you you're wrong. I personally recognize I must grow as a writer. It is a continual, never-ending process, and surprisingly one I look forward to.

STEP FOUR: Just write. When I first started out, it took much longer to get each chapter in decent shape. Since those days, I've grown as a writer and found I can do things much faster. Perhaps it's just that, between my editors and agent, they've pushed me to be stronger at my craft. I think there is some truth to this thought.

I get asked quite a lot what it's like being a full-time author.

"It's great. I only work half days," I say, "twelve hours a day, every day."

My wife finds my answer somewhat amusing. The reality is, she understands the truth in what I'm saying. People who don't know me wonder if I'm being honest. I assure you I am.

To be successful at writing, you need to put in the time, each and every day. It's not easy being an author, but it's even harder being a bestselling author, because you must keep cranking out hits. You are only as good as your last book, and sales in today's marketplace tend to fall off quickly. Hammering out the books takes work and commitment, especially if you want to deliver a quality product.

Most everyone reading this book will not be full-time author, at least not yet. Writing became my profession three years after I published my first book. Honestly, being a full-time author is everything I thought it would be and more. Working from home and the additional time spent with my family makes it worth it. I get to make my own schedule so I can go to special activities and school events now, where before I could hardly ever do so. However, getting to that point, becoming a full-time author, was a struggle.

While working a hectic full-time job, I couldn't realistically put in a twelve-hour day writing. So, you've got to be wondering… how did I write six novels in three years while working a full-time job and successfully running a company to boot? It's back to that mountain analogy again. You work on it every single bloody day, even when you don't want to.

I would come home after a long day at work. I was tired, hungry, and really in no mood to do any additional work. I would play with my kids, have dinner with my family, put my children to bed, and then spend a little time with my wife. She usually goes to bed around 9:30 p.m. From that point until midnight or 1:00 in the morning was my quiet time. That was my sweet spot for writing.

For three years, I survived on very little sleep and lots of coffee. Oh, and I'm also a big believer in naps. If you don't take a nap during the day, you should. Naps are refreshing and help keep you energized. I also caught up on sleep over the weekends.

Now, I had a very high stress job, and writing was, in a way, my escape. For a few hours each night, I was able to plunge into this amazing world that I was building. I could push the headaches of the office aside, if only for a short while.

I can't tell you I worked every single night from the time my wife went to sleep until the wee hours of the morning. Some days, I just didn't have the energy. But what I did do was put in an effort each and every day, even the weekends.

That daily effort might have only been thirty minutes, or an hour, or more. What I found was that, by working on my book a little bit each day, somehow, someway I managed to climb that mountain and complete my novel.

A fundamental process to writing is to keep at it until the job is done. When my agent sends me an email, it doesn't display her name in the sender line. It reads: Just write. She's sending a simple and yet profound message that a lot of people just don't get. Heed it well... and just write.

> RECAP: I approach my writing in a precise and detailed manner. By being organized from the beginning with an outline, I am able to deliver a quality and well-thought-out end product.
>
> Marc's Writing Method in Steps:
>
> 1. Come up with a cool and exciting Idea. Don't share it.
> 2. Develop an outline/story blueprint. Such an approach helps to defeat writer's block.
> 3. Write from beginning to end without editing. Keep the creativity flowing. Edit/improve your story once you have a complete product.
> 4. Put in the time by working towards your goal every single day. Just write.
>
> A fundamental process to writing is simply to keep at it, day after day, and not get sidetracked. What is important is putting in the effort on a daily basis. Thirty minutes here, an hour there, four hours, whatever... your effort adds up over time.
>
> Block time out of your busy schedule to work on your writing. Do whatever keeps you moving forward towards your goal. By attacking a project in such a way, eventually you will climb the mountain and finish.

Chapter Three

The Editing Matters • Different Types of Editing
• Being Open to Feedback • Agents

Bottom Line: The editing matters.

There is a difference between an author and a writer. An author is someone who hasn't given up, a person who perseveres through the terrible writing, the frustration, and the agony of creativity. So, my advice to you once again: "Never give up, never surrender."

Marc's Rule: No book is ever finished; it is only abandoned.

That said, I'm about to tell you to give up. Nothing that you write, as I have already said, is ever going to be perfect. There comes a point when it is good, and by good, I mean ready to pass on to the editor. No book is ever finished; it is only abandoned. That's been one of my favorite axioms. If you strive toward perfection, you just won't get there.

I have readers tell me that my writing is just as good as Tom Clancy, Brandon Sanderson, Tolkien, the list goes on. You can look through my reviews and see the comparisons for yourself. Having read those authors' books, like *Red*

Storm Rising, *The Way of Kings*, and *The Hobbit*, I can tell you that I know, personally, my writing is not as good as theirs. But it's not my opinion that matters. The only opinion that truly counts is the reader's. That is very important for you to remember. You are writing for your audience. I cannot stress enough what this means to building your author platform.

It's incumbent upon you as a writer to give your audience what they want—even if they don't know what they want until they read it. Sounds like stereo instructions, doesn't it?

The more books I publish, the more feedback I get from readers, and the more I understand about the audience reading my books. That helps me fine-tune, refine, and drill down so that what I write continues to appeal to that audience and, more importantly, grows it.

The caution here is to write the very best book you can, but not to get caught in the trap of perfection. I feel like I can always tweak and improve my books to make them better. Remember, no good book is ever finished... it's abandoned. My books will never be good enough for me, but for many of my readers, they will be cherished works, which they will read over and over and over again.

I can't tell you how humbling it is to have people love my work. It's been over four years since I published my first book and it still does not seem real. I've highlighted my successes in this book to show you my path to bestsellers, but I don't think of myself as a bestselling author. Strange, huh?

I make a point to read each review posted on Amazon, Goodreads, or Audible. I read the negative ones, too. If somebody bought my book and cared enough to leave a review, even if it's a one-star, I feel compelled to show them the same respect that they showed me by purchasing my book. I want to hear what they have to say.

I value all reviews, including the ones as an author you don't want to get. Don't let the bad reviews bother you. If you publish a book and put yourself out there, it is a certainty you will get negative reviews. You are vulnerable and readers will judge your work. There is, however, something to be gained from less than stellar reviews. This is different than listening to naysayers. Here you are listening to reader feedback. It is an important distinction and even more critical to understand what they are telling you.

If you keep getting reviews that tell you the book needs an editor, well maybe…just maybe you need a better editor or the book requires more work. If reviewers complain about the writer going on and on and on—spending pages to describe a chair or the grain of the wood of a table—you might want to pay attention to that, too. Just saying.

With all reviews, your readers are telling you something. You, as the author, must decide whether you agree. If you do, or what they're saying seems to make some sense to you, it may be worth your while to go ahead and make changes or modifications to your book.

Just because you published it doesn't mean your work is done. Don't be afraid of going back and fixing things, like mistakes or misspellings, to improve the experience for future readers. Remember, the goal here is to make you a successful author by building your brand. You can't do that if the book is flawed.

Listening and absorbing feedback can be incredibly difficult. If you want to be successful in this marketplace, you need to be able to take feedback, especially from your readers.

The improvement process:
The improvement process is a critical phase of your writing. It's where you take the rough draft or manuscript and make it better. Sounds simple, right? But it isn't.

I take many hours to edit each chapter. It usually works out to around three to four days of work per chapter. It can take as many as seven days for me to reach the point where I feel comfortable that the work on a given chapter is good. This is dependent upon such things as size or complexity of the chapter. But three to four days is a good rule of thumb for me. That gives me a working estimate of how long it will take me until the book will be at a point where I can hand it off to my developmental editor.

So, for example, if I outlined a book with a length of twenty chapters, it takes me twenty days to write from beginning to end as long as I write one chapter per day. Once I have my completed product, then I know, at worst case if it takes me an average of four days to improve each chapter, it will take me roughly around another eighty days of work to improve the book enough to hand off to my developmental editor.

This information is important because it allows me to not only plan out my writing calendar, but also schedule editors and set deadlines and tentative publication dates. This allows me to reverse engineer each book's publication schedule, create a marketing plan, lay out promotions, and figure out my budgetary needs.

If you are working a full-time job, then it will most likely take you longer. That's okay. Your goal should be getting your novel in the best shape as possible and that means setting realistic goals. Don't rush it. If your dream is to be a full-time author, then take the time to do it right from the beginning.

I tell prospective writers this next advice all the time. Most authors only get one chance to introduce themselves and make a splash. Once you've done a belly flop in the proverbial publishing pool, you may not get another opportunity for the perfect dive.

Should your book prove flawed—for example, it has more than a few basic grammatical errors or some parts don't flow logically—your readers will castigate you in their reviews. They will be irritated that they spent good hard-earned cash on a subpar book. More importantly, they will let everyone else know about it. Get enough negative reviews and people will stop buying your book. Reviews matter. It's that simple.

Marc's Rule: No one will care more about your work than you will.

All successful authors I know hired an editor to help them improve their book. This is a good first step for anyone. However, for several struggling authors I've met, it also proved to be a misstep. How can you go wrong hiring an editor? Very easily.

They assumed that once they had gone through the editor's edits and suggested improvements, their book was done and ready to go. Or worse, they simply hit "accept all changes" and did not do a complete read-through of the editor's suggestions as a final stage or formal review. Their thinking in this was that the editor is the professional and must have been right.

I can tell you for fact that when you get your book back from the edit, you are far from done. It is most definitely not ready to publish, even if you "accept all changes." You, as the author, must be involved from not only the very beginning of the process, but to the bitter end and then beyond.

The simple reason for this is that even after the developmental and copy editors get through with your book, there will still be mistakes. No matter how many times it's been edited, or how much the manuscript has been eyeballed by multiple people, there will still be errors: misspelled, misused, and even missing words.

The important takeaway here is limiting basic errors, so they are few and far between. Grammatical errors take the reader out of the story. The more errors, the more the story is interrupted. That translates directly into fewer readers willing to forgive you for a handful of mistakes. Trust me on this. There are people out there who think they are critics on par with Siskel and Ebert. They are more than prepared to tear your book apart in a review. Stay involved to the bitter end and then beyond.

Marc's Rule: Your book should be as polished as possible, before you even hand it off to your editor.

There are more than a few authors who just write a first draft, give it a cursory review, and then hand the book off to the editor to make it better. In short, they are delegating the responsibility of the improvement phase to their editors. That works for them, but I'm not sure in the long run if it's truly working to their benefit. What do I mean by this? Simply put, I do not believe this makes the final product better. In fact, I am of the strong opinion the book will not be as good as it could have been because you are the creative genius behind your book's storyline.

Ever read the first couple books in a series and they're so awesome you can't wait to read the rest, then you're disappointed to discover the quality of the writing drops dramatically in subsequent books? I call this Lazy Author Syndrome. Don't you just hate that? The author feels they've made it big and, going forward, doesn't want to work so hard.

"My fans don't care," one author said, "they'll read anything I write."

This author was wildly successful a few years back. He did not feel he needed a good editor. Now, he knows different. His tune has since changed.

Each book should be special and come from the heart. I'm serious when I say this. Every book I write is important to me. I want it to be the best that it can be. That's why I make sure—no, let me correct that—I make damn certain my work is in the best shape possible before I hand it off to my editor.

Why do I do that? It's simple. I don't want my developmental editor spending her time doing line edits on my work. All editors will see a rough passage or several lines that don't flow particularly well and will go ahead and rewrite that passage. But what I'm really looking for with my developmental editor is for her to help me take my book to the next level. I want her to tell me where the story is weak, where I can increase the stakes, point out when my main character shows too much weakness or goes out of character, etc.

Your editor should help you take your manuscript and make it into a really good book, perhaps even excellent. You would be surprised how many authors and writers are unable to absorb or even hear critical feedback without getting emotional. If you listen and are open and logical in your analysis of professional feedback, then perhaps together you might be able to bring your manuscript to the next level. Nothing grows your author platform faster than an awesome book.

Remember, you are writing for your audience. They want a great book. Why settle for average when you can give them what they want?

In short, I badly want my developmental editor to focus on the developmental part of my story. I want her looking at the plot, character arcs, the arc of the story itself, point of view, narrative, themes, voice, etc. I don't want her spending too much time on line edits. There is only so much time that she has with the book, and I want to maximize that.

I think I have been somewhat successful at this. But I know that, as a writer, I have room to grow, and with each book I learn. My writing gets better and better. As you progress as a writer, your goal should not be simply to keep pumping out books. It should be to improve as a writer, to grow. If you do, your readership will grow with you, and so too will your author platform.

Marc's rule: You need to be open to feedback.

This is quite possibly the most fundamental facet of writing, at least in my opinion. You need to be open to feedback, particularly from your editors. If you can't take feedback, you shouldn't be a writer. It is that simple. By nature, any writer is subject to their worst nightmare: the critic. And guess what? Everyone out there who reads your work is, to one degree or another, a critic.

Your first feedback on any project generally will and should come from an editor. As such, it is important to understand the different types of edits. When I published my first book, I did not know the difference between a developmental and copy edit. After I picked up my agent, she was kind enough to explain the difference and why it was important. Let me tell you, I needed to know the difference.

Up until that point, my first book's run had been wildly successful. However, as the sales continued to roll in, I started getting complaints from readers, both in reviews and messaging, that I needed my book to be better edited. There were lots of little errors sprinkled throughout. The book had been edited; however, it needed additional work, and from a sentence-level perspective, I had a lot to learn. Thankfully, my agent was there to help.

She found me an awesome developmental editor, someone who had extensive experience in my genre and, more importantly, understood fantasy. And at the same time, my agent also recommended an incredible copy editor.

In addition to that, my agent also edits my work and gives me her thoughts. She has a lifetime of experience in the publishing world and has helped me skyrocket to success as a full-time author.

So… what does a developmental editor do?

A developmental editor looks at your story as a whole. They pay attention to character arcs, motivations, and voice within the story. They aim to improve the content and structure of your work. Developmental editors tackle such things as plot, characterization, pacing, and setting. These are not little things. They are critically important to your story, and a good editor will help make your book stronger.

I've had many… many… so many… I've forgotten how many conversations with authors who are struggling to make a splash. When I look up their books on Amazon, I typically see their average rating being around 3 stars. There is usually a common theme with the reviews. The author needs an editor.

It is either that or there are only a handful of reviews, with a 4 to 4.5 star average. Usually 50% of the reviews are from people the author knows. The other half of the reviews are mediocre in their praise of the book. That's generally a sign the reason the book did not take off was the story was not gripping enough.

When I recommend to these authors that they go out and find a good or better editor to either help them smooth things out or add a little spice, I get excuses or comments from them that they've already had their book edited or they had a bad experience with their editor. There is not a willingness on their part to listen to what I have to say to help them. They are close-minded and that is primarily the problem.

"The editor just did not get my book." This generally means one of two things:

    A. The developmental editor they chose might not edit books in their genre.
    B. The author cannot handle critical feedback.

Both are common problems, and both are fixable, if the author desires.

On the developmental side, you have an opportunity to search out an editor you feel comfortable working with. You don't have to work with the very first person you run into. A key question, if you're writing a science fiction book, would be to ask the editor how many science fiction works he or she has edited. Simple question, right? It will tell you a lot right off the bat about the editor's experience.

Marc's Rule: Find an editor who has experience editing in your genre.

If the editor tells you they've only ever edited mystery or historical fiction books, they might not be the right choice for you. If their passion is science fiction, well then, maybe they are the one for you and the rest is destiny.

Don't be afraid to ask for references. Speak with authors they've worked with. I strongly encourage you to do so. Pick up that phone and call those references. Typically, authors will tell you honestly what they think of their editor. In my experience, they will tell you the editor's weaknesses and strengths. This is important because if you choose to work with that person…you need to know where to pay special attention. It is up to you to choose the right editor. This is not an easy decision and should not be made lightly. A good editor can make or break your book.

Having chosen an editor, it is important to listen to their feedback. This is perhaps one of the greatest failings of most struggling authors. They are incapable of hearing any type of critical feedback on their work. I get it. I struggle with this myself.

When I finished *The Tigers Time*, a massive tome over 227,000 words, I did not want to hear any critical feedback on my book. I was tired and exhausted, ready to close that project. I wrote this book in just four and a half months. But guess what? Despite the exhaustion and weariness for the project, I made sure to listen and think on the feedback.

It turned out there was a problem with the beginning of my book. My editor pointed it out to me and I made the appropriate changes. The end result was a better book. As a writer, and as an author, you need to be open to critical feedback. Do not make the mistake of reacting instantly when you receive feedback. An editor is not criticizing your book just because they can. Under no circumstances should you take it personally. They are giving you their *professional* opinion and, with it, suggestions to help improve and bring the story to the next level.

When your manuscript is returned from the editor, there will literally be thousands of suggested changes and corrections. How do you approach this overwhelming level of feedback? I typically go through and address the line edits and basic fixes first. This usually takes me around two to four hours and cleans up the manuscript nicely.

I don't pay any attention to the developmental edits until I am done with the basic fixes. Only then will I read through the suggested edits and my editor's notes. Once I'm done, I close the document, turn off the computer, and walk away.

For the rest of the night, I won't focus on writing. I will spend time with my family, watch TV, go out to a movie, or play a game. I intentionally put space between me and the work, to allow the editorial feedback to sink in. The next day, first thing, I will make myself a coffee, sit down, and only then begin tackling those pesky and frustrating developmental edits... knocking out one at a time.

It is these suggested edits that take the most time and occasionally will require you to rewrite a chapter or section of your manuscript. It is important that you think logically and not emotionally about what the editor is saying. There is a tremendous temptation to react with anger or frustration. This is especially true when the editor is telling you some portion of your book just isn't working or is confusing, the motivation of a character is off, or you need to increase the stakes... whatever it is that needs improvement.

The frustration and anger manifest themselves because it means you will be required to spend additional time working on a story you thought was finished. I've been there. The last thing you want to hear is that more work is required. It may not be what you want, but it's what you need to hear. This is usually the time when my best work is done and my manuscript goes from good to really good.

I'm not saying that you have to agree with everything the editor suggests. There are certain times when they're wrong or, as the author, you just feel the suggestion made will not work. Remember, you have the final say. With that ultimate decision also comes great responsibility.

A cautionary note here. If you disregard good advice because it's too much work or you're just plain wrong, that might mean your book ends up being not as good or as polished as it could have been. Ultimately, it is your book and final decisions or changes need to feel right to you. However, you have to live with the consequences of such decisions, because an average-to-substandard book will not help you build your author platform. It will hurt it and set a writing career back. Publishing is a harsh world and it's best to understand that now.

What is a copy editor?
A copy editor is someone whose specific focus is to make sure that your word usage and punctuation is correct and in the right place, along with many other things such as formatting being consistent, etc. A great copy editor will ensure you don't make simple errors and, believe me, as a writer, you will. It's part of the business. No one is perfect. Such an editor will help you catch little errors and omissions, making your work that much better, polished, and clean.

Getting your manuscript copy edited is an important and necessary step for all books. If your word usage is off and incorrect, you will get lambasted by reviewers. I've run into struggling authors, looking to save a buck, who think their own copy editing skills are more than enough to muddle through. Don't make the same mistake. Grammar and word usage is constantly in flux and ever changing. Professional editors help authors keep on top of such changes. Keep in mind, language is fluid and at times terribly complex.

What kinds of errors and omissions am I talking about?

Example One: *Stiger climbed steps.* The line should have read, *Stiger climbed up the steps.* I missed the words: *up the.* My copy editor caught it.

Example Two: *The king tugged on the reigns of his horse.* The correct word usage is *reins*.
I did not have *Stiger's Tigers* copy edited. Not because I was looking to skimp and save money, but because I did not know what a copy editor was or, more importantly, why I needed one. Example Two was a mistake I made in the first version of *Stiger's Tigers*. I got hammered on it by a number of reviewers who complained in their reviews. Don't make the same mistake I did. Get a copy editor.

It is vitally important you choose the right editors for you. Make sure that they are people who you can work with, but more importantly, be certain they understand the genre you're writing in.

To get a proofreader or not to get a proofreader? That is the question.

There is also a third stage of the editing, or really the finishing process. This is called proofreading. You can easily hire a proofreader. I don't myself, as my books are typically edited twice by the developmental editor, once by my agent, and then by my copy editor. In addition to that lengthy process, I have at least twenty beta readers, who are super fans that also read through multiple early versions of the manuscript. By the time it comes to the endgame, my novels are well-polished.

Instead of hiring a proofreader, I do the proofreading myself. The reason I take the time to do it is that nobody cares about your work more than you do. Typically, I will read the book two or three times after I get it back from the copy editor. By this point in the process, my eyeballs hurt and I hate the story with a passion. But I will not delegate this task to anyone else. It is that important to me.

Hate, you say? It's more of a pure loathing at this stage in the game. Think about it this way. For the last eighty days, all I've been doing is spending my time improving the manuscript to the point where it's good enough to go to the developmental editor. Then it comes back for review.

I've gone over all the changes and suggestions and made the fixes I feel are appropriate. I read the manuscript again to make certain there are no major issues. If I feel the book does not need another developmental edit, I send it off to my beta readers and at the same time to my copy editor. While they have the book, I begin reading it over and over and over again. I do this to make sure I've not missed anything, like basic plot mistakes. I want everything to feel just right.

When the manuscript comes back from the copy editor and my betas, I usually have a few dozen changes myself to make. Then I'll go through the corrections on the copy edit. When that's all done, I read the manuscript again and then yet again, combing line by line … searching for any last mistakes and errors to eliminate before the book goes off for formatting and ultimately publishing. So, hate at this point is an appropriate word.

If you're not good at proofing your own work, then I recommend a proofreader. It will save you grief from poor reviews and there is a good chance that will translate into additional sales. Even if you engage a proofreader, do a final read-through yourself. When you publish, your book should be in the best shape possible. If I sound like a broken record, it's because I am trying to hammer this point home.

There are other types of editors. You can look them up. However, in my opinion, the three I mentioned above are the most important for self-publishing fiction.

Marc's Rule: If you want the job done right, you are going to have to pay for it.

Paying for everything. All this sounds pricey, right? How much does it cost?

You're gonna have to pay for it, if you want the job done right. I would not recommend publishing a book without having it developmentally edited and copy edited. I've heard horror stories of authors paying $10,000 or more to have their manuscript edited. If you're paying that much money as a first-time author, I feel comfortable saying that you are getting ripped off.

You can easily find a good developmental editor for a fraction of that cost. Of course, this all depends upon the size of your book, experience level of the editor, scope of the project, and length of time required to edit. These things can all impact the cost. I recommend that you shop around, not only for the best fit, but for a price you can afford.

The big traditional publishers have gotten into the game of supporting self-published authors. You have to watch out for your interests with whoever you choose to work with—big, small, or independent press.

Many of the big publishers will provide publishing services to Indie authors for a price. I encourage you to research this option. I personally have never worked with a traditional publisher on the self-publishing side.

There is, of course, the comfort of going with a traditional publisher for self-publishing, as opposed to working with the small or Indie press to handle your formatting or perhaps even your editing. I would recommend you find the editor that is the best fit for you. Don't go to a publisher and automatically take their recommended editor. Remember, you also want to talk to that person prior to engaging their services and ask for references. Until you search around, you won't be prepared to make an informed decision.

Marc's Rule: If I can do it, you can too!

Can you publish a book yourself?
Of course you can. In today's marketplace you're able to manage every single step in the process. Thanks to Amazon, Barnes & Noble, and other platforms, authors can self-publish their books. You can put yourself out there without ever having to go through a traditional publisher or agent.

How cool is that?
Amazon is literally my favorite company. You won't hear this from traditional publishers, but I am a huge fan of what Jeff Bezos has done for the publishing industry. Amazon has changed the game, giving power and new reach to writers. I don't think I would have become a bestselling author had I not self-published with Amazon on the Kindle platform. If I can do it, you can do it. It is as simple as that.

There are several ways to self-publish. As I said, you can go through a big traditional publisher or work with a small/Indie press that focuses exclusively on self-published authors. In both cases you should retain the rights to your books and not have to sign or lease away the ultimate ownership. You can even do everything yourself.

Unless you're a tech-savvy person, I would not recommend that last option. However, there are tools out there you can use to help you format your books, guide you through the design of your book cover, and generally allow you to publish your book yourself, at a significant savings. As I said, I don't recommend this approach unless you absolutely have to.

Just keep in mind that, whatever you choose to do, you must make your decisions wisely. If you make a mistake at any stage, it will have consequences and, more than likely, the people reading your book will leave negative reviews. That's why it is important to have a professional handle the formatting and layout for your book.

Whether it is a small press or a large one, a professional who does this day in and day out and knows exactly what they're doing is less likely to make critical mistakes. They should get everything right. Look at it this way: Say you fall ill and need an important surgery. Do you want to go to a doctor who does that specific surgery once in a great while or go to a surgeon who performs that same surgery several times per week and is considered an expert in their field?

Unless you have a lot of images or charts, it shouldn't cost you a lot of money to get a book formatted for eBook and print on demand. I want you to be aware that self-publishing is not cheap, but if you do it correctly, you have a better chance at earning a decent return on your investment.

Remember to plan ahead and put money away for the services you will need. Budget according to the fees your selected providers charge so that you can be prepared. When creating a timeline, be certain to include estimated dates and amounts of expenses you will need to pay out.

I recently read an article that shared that the average self-published author makes less than $1,000 a year. More importantly, nearly 35% of all Indie authors pull in less than $500 a year. That is a staggering figure. Don't believe me? Look it up yourself. When you look at the expense to self-publish, not to mention the time invested in writing the book, for some people it does not make the effort worth it. That is why you must pay attention to every single stage of the process and why you have to look at publishing as a business or an investment.

There is no excuse for not being involved in every step, from concept, to writing, to editing, to proofing, to marketing. Direct involvement is essential to brand building. If you are successful at growing your author platform, you should be able to exceed what the average author pulls in and increase the chances of building a successful writing career.

Unfortunately, not everyone reading this book will be successful. There are just so many pitfalls in this industry that, sadly, it is the exception that succeeds. Very few authors strike gold from random luck alone. It takes work and I can't stress this enough. If you are looking for an easy job, being an author is not it.

Do you need an agent to self-publish?
The short answer is no. In today's market, it's harder and harder to get an agent in general fiction. If you can put up big numbers as a self-published author, they will become more interested, but it's still difficult to find an agent. In addition, many traditional publishers don't accept unagented manuscripts.

The job of agents has historically been to sell their authors' books to traditional publishing houses. The change in the market has seen the agent's role begin to change too, where many now work closely with successful Indie authors. My recommendation is that you find one that you can work with. However, the problem is that most agents won't be interested in what you have to offer unless you've already established yourself in the marketplace and achieved some measure of success.

That's kind of unfair, but guess what? That's just how it is. Literary agents get bombarded by emails from prospects. They have perhaps three or four seconds to consider each email before hitting the delete button. That sucks. But that's reality. You have to work in the environment that you're given. It's breaking out that sets you apart from the rest and gets an agent's attention.

I broke out from the pack and lucked out by finding my literary agent. At the time, *Stiger's Tigers* was seeing considerable success. I was being approached by agents seeking to represent me. One agent suggested that I pay him to represent me and he would find me a book deal. That seemed unprofessional. So, I wrote several literary agencies directly. I asked them whether or not it made sense for me to be represented. One agent wrote me back.

She advised me that she was no longer taking on any new authors but would be willing to have a conversation over the phone and give me some advice. We set up a call, and unbeknownst to me, she had picked up my first book and read it before we talked.

We had a wonderful conversation and she gave me some great advice. In addition to that, she told me she would be interested in representing me, but I had to work with her to improve my writing. Working with her entailed listening objectively to her advice and guidance. I thought, Okay, this sounds good.

The next thing she told me was that I needed to change the end of *Stiger's Tigers*. At the time, I had just wrapped up writing *The Tiger* and I was exhausted. This was also due in part because I was working a full-time job. Needless to say, it was the last thing I wanted to hear. *Stiger's Tigers* was already a runaway success. I asked her why it needed to be changed. In less than forty-five seconds, she explained to me where I had gone wrong.

More important, she didn't sugarcoat. I sat there in my chair and thought, Holy shit, she's right. I told her I would make the changes. I would commit to sign with her if she would provide me references for authors she was currently working with. She provided the references and after I called and spoke with them, I was convinced that she was the agent for me.

Over the past four years, seeing nine books published, my agent has proven to be an invaluable ally in not only building my author platform, but in making my writing career successful. My agent and my editors have taken my writing to a whole new level. I feel like she's on my side, but unfortunately, there are agents out there who are only looking out for themselves and don't care about the authors they represent. You want to avoid these kind of people. A good way to do that is by checking references.

So, yes, I think having an agent is good idea. However, in most instances you will need to establish yourself as an author and build your brand first so that you can get the attention of those agents. But when you're able to do so, don't go with the first agent you run into, at least not without talking to their references. There are plenty of unscrupulous people out there who will act in their own interest first and yours second... if you are lucky.

Please, please talk to several agents before making a final choice on who you want to represent you. It is a big, big decision and one that can't be backed out of easily.

Good agents are worth their weight in gold. I know for a fact that my agent is one of the keys to my success. Yes, it took a lot of work, but she helped me grow my sales from 25,000 books to over 180,000+ within a few short months of signing with her. I would not have been able to do it without her. If you find a good agent, listen to them.

Marc's Rule: Never begrudge a good agent their commission.

Keep in mind that a good agent wants you to be successful. That is their focus and business. Most are literary professionals with years of experience behind them. They will make suggestions based upon their highly specialized experience, which most of you reading this book will not have. Heck, I've only been published since 2015 and I'm still learning the intricacies of the business. While I firmly believe anyone can learn it alone, having an agent as an advocate and mentor for me has streamlined the process exponentially.

You should listen with an open mind when your agent suggests something. If your sales increase, not only will you make more money, but your agent will earn more money too. It's their business to guide your career and they should be laser focused on helping you achieve a high level of success. If you are successful, they are successful. Difficult clients who don't listen, are overly concerned about money, fight with publishers, or resist good advice tend to struggle. They wonder why they are not getting the big money-making deals and why their agent stops returning calls. Could there be a correlation here?

Let me tell you something else: I am incredibly pleased that my agent makes a percentage of whatever I sell, because she has earned every single percentage point. 15% is the standard in the industry and agents don't earn a salary. Both of our paychecks are sales-driven. Never begrudge a good agent for making money off your work. Don't get greedy and lose sight of the difference they can make.

RECAP: Editing matters.

1. Hire professionals, including a developmental and a copy editor.
2. Find editors who are a good fit and have experience in the genre you are writing.
3. Be open to feedback.
4. Stay involved till publication and after. No one will care more about your work than you.
5. Your book should be as polished as possible. Limit the number of basic errors, otherwise your reviews will suffer.
6. To do everything right, it is going to cost.
7. An agent can make all the difference as an advocate and mentor. However, in today's market, you will likely need to establish yourself first, just to catch their attention.

Chapter Four

To Self-Publish or Not • Traditional Publishing vs. Indie
• The Advantages of Amazon & Kindle Unlimited

Bottom Line: To self-publish or not to self-publish?

This book is focused almost exclusively on self-publishing fiction and particularly on the Amazon platform. It's where my direct experience and success lie. I haven't gone down the traditional route as of yet. As such, I can't give you a personal feel from traditional publishing, but I can share with you some of what I've learned by self-publishing my own books.

I've had several opportunities to present and sell to traditional publishers, but up until this point I have declined to move forward, primarily due to the freedom that comes with being an Indie. I am sure in the near future I will ink a deal with a publisher for a series. It's a way to further grow my author platform and expose my writing to new readers, those who patron the brick-and-mortar stores along with libraries. At this point in my career, it seems to make good business sense. So, let's take a moment and examine some of the basic mechanics, moving parts, and differences between self- and traditional publishing.

With traditional publishers, authors typically get paid twice a year. With a traditional publisher, there is a very detailed agreement with numerous provisions that are important to understand. You want to carefully read through any publishing agreement if you are lucky enough to land a deal.

A good agent should be able to negotiate any troublesome provisions out of a contract. Of course, this also depends upon how badly the publisher wants to work with the author. If they're taking what they consider to be a risk, they may insist on certain provisions to protect themselves.

Either way, this is one of the reasons you get an agent. They have the experience to help spot any red flags. Agents are great at navigating the complicated field of subrights such as audio, foreign rights, film/TV, etc. Think of an agent as your experienced business partner, but they are not an attorney.

Marc's Rule: It is better to be educated than ignorant.

Not only should the author review any publishing agreement, but it is also my personal recommendation that you hire a literary attorney to review any and all contracts. The Author's Guild has some great resources. They provide a lot of information and free consultations, along with a directory of literary attorneys for hire. An attorney may charge a few hundred or more dollars for a contract review.

I can't stress enough how important it is to get agreements professionally reviewed. Between an attorney and an agent, they should be able to point out any sticky issues, such as ownership of the work, net profits vs. gross profits, non-compete language, licensing, subsidiaries, payment schedules, revised edition clauses...the list goes on. It is better to be educated than ignorant so that you fully understand what you are committing yourself to.

Typically, there are a few rounds of negotiations to secure a deal. Don't be afraid to ask for things you want included or removed from an agreement. This is your business and your passion. You should not only want to make money, but also protect your interests.

Speak up for yourself. The worst they can say is no when you ask for a change or modification of contract language. If they do, well then, it's time to decide how badly you want or need the book deal.

Royalties are another tricky area in publishing contracts. Per book, they are much less than you would get being a self-published author, typically around 12–15%. That doesn't mean you can't make money with a traditional publisher. Get the right one and they can be a marketing machine, reaching a large audience of readers, too, just a different kind—primarily those who frequent the bookstore or prefer a book in hand.

I know several authors who make a very good living going that route. However, I think that they are the exception, as opposed to the rule. This point is the same for both self-publishing and traditional authors: Some authors make a good living and some make buckets of money, but most don't make much at all.

Another potential issue in going with a traditional publisher is the length of time to publication. You're not their only author. Most publishers have set production schedules that are booked months, sometimes years, in advance. They essentially have a backlog of books to print, ship to stores, and market with carefully coordinated campaigns. This all takes time, especially fitting a new, unproven author into the schedule. It could mean a serious delay from manuscript delivery to publication, perhaps as long as twenty-four months or more.

The publisher may also decide your book is not up to snuff and want you to make changes before they publish. That also takes time and can make the process even lengthier. You might get your full advance but be forced to wait for the book to publish and start selling enough copies to earn back the advance through book sales before you begin getting paid regularly. That process might take a year or more from publication, if it ever happens.

This isn't good news, right? I am giving it to you straight and pointing out the worst case. There are plenty of authors who've had a great experience going the traditional route. Still, I think it is better to be educated than ignorant of what could await.

When it comes to self-publishing with Amazon or the other platforms available, you retain tremendous control over your own product. Not only are you able to have your book formatted in less than two weeks for eBook and print on demand (POD), but you can publish almost immediately, when it's ready.

Self-published authors generally get paid monthly, as opposed to annually or biannually with a traditional publisher. The royalties on Amazon's KDP platform can be as high as 70% for eBook, with a low of 35%. This is dependent upon the price the author sets and the platform selected.

When it comes to print on demand, you'll generally make less per book than eBook, but again, you retain the control and freedom to set the price. Income on POD is generally dependent upon the size of the book and, like eBook, the author can select the price point.

With a traditional publisher, they basically own the book, though in truth they are technically leasing the rights. The copyright always belongs to the author, unless the writer is working for hire. Still, you will have little control over price, promotions, or marketing plans. The publisher takes that over completely, though in today's ever-changing marketplace, publishers are increasingly turning to authors for marketing and self-promotion. That's why the author's platform becomes so important when pitching books.

Self-published authors often won't see their books in brick-and-mortar bookstores, although it can happen if the book is a runaway success. Why is that? Bookstores typically do not have the ability to return self-published books that don't sell, like they do with a traditional publisher. In addition, the discounts provided by traditional publishers are greater than POD, which translates into a larger revenue share for the bookstore.

Publishers also pay for placement and visibility. Understand that revenue drives business decisions, and shelving traditionally published books essentially becomes the path of least resistance for the big retail box shops. All that said, it may be worth it for Indie authors to reach out to local bookstores and libraries to see if they can get their book on the shelf. Many smaller bookstores make an effort to carry local authors.

A self-published book faces an uphill battle in the bookstore, and for a self-published author it is not the best place to fight for sales. Amazon and other online platforms allow you to compete for readers in a more dynamic and fluid environment. The self-published author even has direct control over promotions, marketing, and sales decisions, something key to building your author platform.

In the end, you must decide for yourself which is the best long-term route to go. I personally prefer the monthly payments associated with self-publishing. It's like getting a regular paycheck, especially important when you're just getting started. Another advantage is that Amazon, through their Kindle Direct Publishing (KDP) website, provides you with critical data that is broken out daily and to the hour. I am not talking about the marketing reports, but the main reporting package KDP provides in relation to daily and monthly sales. It takes experience to read and understand them. However, once you become familiar with how it works, the reporting can be an incredibly useful tool.

At any given time, the author can see the number of eBooks and print books sold, along with how many Kindle Unlimited page reads for the day. You don't have to agonize about whether or not a book is selling. All you need do is log into the KDP site and see for yourself. You will know what your income for the current month is likely to be in a matter of seconds. With a traditional publisher, the author must wait for their reporting, which arrives around the time they pay you.

Amazon's KDP reporting is an incredibly powerful tool that should not be underestimated. It allows the savvy author to experiment with marketing techniques in near real-time to find out what works and what doesn't.

So yes, I am a huge—and I mean *huge*—fan of Amazon. They provide lots of analytical reporting information and pay monthly. I've never had a serious problem with them paying royalties. The only downside is you don't get an advance. But honestly, who needs one when you are paid regularly, don't have to wait months to publish, and are a successful author?

Amazon upset the apple cart, and it shows. The traditional publishers are struggling to compete, as Amazon has drawn millions of readers away from the brick-and-mortar bookstores to their Kindle and Audible platforms, along with being an online marketplace for print books. These readers now shop in an online bookstore with millions of titles readily available, at the click of a button.

But self-publishing is not all peaches and cream. Many authors struggle to get noticed or even to generate sales. Remember that statistic I mentioned that most self-published authors make less than $1,000 a year? Don't believe me? Look it up. Being a self-published author is hard. I recall Kermit the Frog saying, "It's not easy being green." Well... it's not easy making the green.

Amazon has, in my humble opinion, the best algorithm out there, or artificial intelligence, when it comes to selling books both online and POD. The algorithm is very good at figuring out what types of books readers are likely to buy.

Anyone who tells you they know exactly how that algorithm works is lying to you, and such claims should be treated with a grain of salt. The algorithm is secret and constantly learning from readers' behaviors and patterns. In other words, it is continually changing. It is a continual work in progress.

Having published with Amazon for years and utilized their built-in advertising, I like to think I have a little more visibility than most, but even I don't fully understand how their algorithm works. It's just how it is. Remember, Amazon is a business. They want to sell stuff, your book included. Their algorithm is designed to do that, to help customers find what they're looking for fast and with fewer clicks of a button. The algorithm will make recommendations to that customer, and in turn, those consumers will find more and more products that fit their needs.

The more of any given product they sell, the more the algorithm grants you some love. Amazon rewards success. It will show your novel to readers who have purchased books like yours. Think of it as a game of anticipating what the buyer wants and then showing it to them. If the customer purchases, you win. Amazon has gotten very good at that.

The algorithm knows every single thing you have ever bought, clicked on, and viewed on any Amazon website. It also takes into account time of day, month, holidays, when you are most likely to buy, and a million other details. Amazon is not just an online store, but also one of the largest search engines in the world. It is designed to help you find what you want, even if you don't quite know what that is yet.

As I understand things…

And keep in mind, by no means am I an expert on Amazon's algorithm, nor do I have inside knowledge. Amazon is a secretive company and they keep this sort of stuff close to their vest. This information comes from what I've read online and directly observed over the years; I could be right and wrong or a mixture of both. I think I'm fairly close to right in my understanding of how the AI works, though.

So, to begin again… as I understand things, if the prospect buys, the algorithm will show your novel to more readers in that same category or demographic and then to some outside of it to determine whether your work has greater appeal.

Should the book stop selling to a market segment or specific demographic in certain categories or receive a negative response (i.e. terrible reviews), Amazon's algorithm will stop showing your book in favor of another author's work to those potential prospects, thus narrowing the amount of people that are exposed to your novel. Translation… fewer sales roll in. That's a very important reason why it is *so* critical to get things right with your manuscript before you publish. It gives your novel a chance to stand out from the crowd, not only by selling, but by getting good reviews, and therefore better placement in Amazon's marketing.

The more people who buy your book, the more Amazon will help you do the heavy lifting and the greater success you will see as the algorithm helps to share the good word about your book.

Then there is Amazon's KDP Select Program and Kindle Unlimited program (KU), a real game changer in the publishing industry. By enrolling your book into Amazon's KDP Select Program you are agreeing to eBook exclusivity with Amazon for a period of 90 days. You cannot sell your eBook elsewhere during this period. In return, Amazon makes your book available to KU subscribers (readers) and you gain two promotional programs to choose between to help build your reader base: Kindle Countdown Deal or Free Promotion.

A Kindle Countdown Deal allows you to discount your book for a set period of time. Prospective readers can see that your book is on sale. A Free Promotion is just what it sounds like, eBooks are given away for free for a set period of time. These are powerful promotional tools and are not to be taken lightly when it comes to building an author platform.

What exactly is KU? This is a subscription service that allows users to access a large selection of books whose authors have agreed to participate in the Kindle Unlimited borrowing program. Users, for a monthly subscription fee, can borrow and read as many eBooks as they want. It is quite a deal, especially if you're a voracious reader. With over one million books enrolled, the program has won a lot of converts—both readers and authors.

Authors participating in the Kindle Unlimited program are paid on a per page basis for books, rather than an upfront percentage for a direct sale. This is a cool service and has seen significant growth since it first launched in

2014. I want to be clear: By participating in this program, your book is still available for direct purchase to those who don't subscribe to KU. Think of it as an additional distribution outlet.

Kindle Unlimited accounts for more than 50% of my sales. It is a program I think worthwhile to participate in for most self-published authors. That said, I know authors who refuse to join the program and loathe it with a passion. For me, KU works out quite well. I am very happy with both KU and Amazon. If you're intent on self-publishing, I would encourage you to enroll your book in the program and try it out. At a minimum, learn more about it.

As I said, by participating in KDP Select, the author is required to offer their eBook exclusively through Amazon for a set period of time. That means you cannot have it available through Barnes & Noble, Smashwords, or any other platform. You must keep it exclusively on Kindle and in the program for 90 days. Three months is not a long time, and if you're unhappy with the results, pull your book out.

There are a number of advantages to participating in KU exclusivity, besides Kindle Countdown Deals and Free Promotions. When you market, you can advertise that your book is available on Amazon, Print, and Kindle Unlimited. What this means is that anyone who sees your advertisement and has a KU subscription understands that they can essentially get the book for free. KU makes it an easy acquisition for them and sales conversion for you.

KU is yet another reason to make sure your book is in the best shape possible prior to publication. The more gripping and error-free, the greater the likelihood that the reader will read on after the first few pages. Remember, with KU, the author is paid on a per page read basis. If the book is poorly done, the KU user is likely to stop reading and move on to another free book. This means the author is losing money and leaving dollars on the table.

There are authors who hate KU and KDP Select. They are convinced enrolling their books into the program, in the end, costs them money. You can go online and do a simple Google search. Read the pros and cons, along with some of the positions that various authors have staked out. Make up your own mind on the issue.

For me, the KU program has opened up an audience I may never have had access to. With over one million books in the KU program, why should a subscriber ever want to purchase your book when they can get plenty of books for free by simply clicking to download?

Try the program. See for yourself if it works for you. I've had readers tell me the only reason they gave me a shot was because my books were enrolled in KU. So, I am a convert and an example of success in KU. It is one of many things to consider on the road to publication.

With your first book, it may be hard to obtain an agent to help you sell your work to a traditional publisher. There are alternate paths to getting an agent, but one possibly open to the Indie author is self-publishing your work. That means getting your book into great shape and launching it with a plan to begin building your author platform.

If you're already self-published, then your focus should be to continue building your author platform to the point where you can get an agent to take notice. Once you secure a quality agent, they can help guide your career to that next level. At that point, you will have more options available to you, including the difficult question of remaining an Indie or switching over to traditional publishing, or a hybrid author who does both.

Both paths have advantages and disadvantages. It will be up to you to choose. You might even be able to dabble in both. I fully intend to.

RECAP: It's better to be educated than not. Learn as much as you can about the route you plan on taking.

1. Understand the difference between the traditional and self-publishing industries/marketplace, including royalty payment frequency and levels. Both paths have advantages and disadvantages. Self-publishing generally pays monthly and at a greater percentage. Don't expect your book to end up in the bookstore.
2. Review agreements carefully. Make certain you understand all provisions and clauses. More importantly, consult a literary attorney to help protect your interests. Stand up for yourself and what you want when it comes to contract negotiations.
3. Understand the basics of Amazon's algorithm and how it can work to help market your book. That's another reason to get your book in as good a shape as possible.
4. Kindle Unlimited compensates on a per page basis and can open you up to a new audience you might not have had access to otherwise.

CHAPTER FIVE

The Essentials Every Author Needs for Marketing Success

Bottom Line: Essential, noun; a thing that is absolutely necessary.

Every author needs the following: Author website, Amazon Author Page/Author Central, newsletter, Goodreads Author Page, Facebook Author Page, Instagram, Twitter, business cards, swag, Booklinker, giveaways/hook books, and a quality book cover.

There are a multitude of essential marketing tools every author should have in place prior to publication. I want to be clear: I do not believe any of these are optional. If you want to build your brand and become a successful author, there are certain things you need to have in place prior to publishing to help make that happen. I have listed them in no particular order. I believe they are all equally valuable and together should help make it easier for the author to build brand and sell books. Ignore them at your peril.

Author Website

An author website is a vital tool to help engage readers. It provides additional information about the author, the books, and writing. I can hear a few of you groaning as I write. A website, really? That must be super expensive and time-consuming. Wrong on both counts. It is relatively easy to set up and not terribly costly, either. It is also a business expense and therefore tax deductible.

Check out my website.
https://www.maenovels.com/

I recommend perusing some of your favorite authors' websites to help give you an idea of the different types of sites out there. Do your homework. Put together a vision of what you would like your website to look like. Choose a theme to match your brand. Find a web developer, one who's not overly expensive, and share those ideas. It's helpful to provide examples and screenshots so that the developer can get a better understanding of what you want and need. Also make a point to listen. Remember, building websites is what they do. All of this should be geared toward engaging readers and helping you build brand.

Always, always, always, whenever hiring someone for a service, ask for references. Have I mentioned this before? In the case of web development, they should share websites they have developed for similar businesses. Judge for yourself whether the firm or person you're thinking about hiring understands your vision and your brand identity. Check their references to confirm the job was done in a timely manner. One thing you want to know is that when changes are required, they get done right away and it doesn't take weeks or months to complete. Some companies even create customizable themes and packages you can purchase for lower rates.

If you're tech savvy, perhaps you can create a simple website yourself for a nominal fee. Personally, I hired someone else to build my website so that I could have more time to focus on my writing. I've enough going on between advertising, actively working to build my brand, and writing. I didn't want any additional work to worry about. My wife, on the other hand, purchased a theme and hired a virtual assistant to set up a few pages on her website when she first started her business. She has since learned how to create new pages and updates her own blog and website so that she doesn't have to pay for these services.

What pages should an author website have?

1. **HOME OR WELCOME PAGE**: This is the landing page where visitors first reach your website. Prominently, it should have the author's name, the cover of the latest novel or an upcoming book highlighted, and a newsletter signup. Efforts should be made to limit the amount of text on this page. You don't want your visitors glazing over because you've written the Magna Carta. Save such text for secondary pages that will allow the reader to become as engaged as they wish.

On my landing page, you will note I have tabs leading to other pages: my name, the cover of the next upcoming book, a little bit of text and, most importantly, a sign-up to my newsletter. There is also a link to my Facebook author page and Twitter, as well as other important links. Facebook is where you should have most of your engagement, so make certain you include that link, too.

2. **ABOUT PAGE**: This page is important because readers visiting the page generally want to learn more about you, the author. Find a good picture of yourself. Post it on this page and write a short biography. No need to run on and on and on. Just the basics. Give the readers a little background on you … the real you. If a reader is hitting this page, you've already impressed them. There is no need to exaggerate.

3. **BOOKS**: This page is where you want to showcase your work. I send prospective readers there all the time. There should be links from this page to book-specific product pages. Since I also have three series, I have an additional tab entitled: WHAT TO READ FIRST. I direct new readers with questions to this page to clear any confusion right up.

4. **APPEARANCES OR EVENTS**: Create this page if you are planning on making any appearances at the local library, fair, conventions, bookstores, or shows so that your readers know where to find you. Every year, I make a point of attending DragonCon. This past year, I had a couple fly in from California to meet me and get a book signed. They told me they did not follow me on Facebook or Twitter but visited my website. It turns out they learned I was going to the convention and thought it would be fun to go and meet me. This was a humbling experience and something I wasn't quite ready for, especially since DragonCon is in Atlanta and they were from California.

5. **INTERVIEWS**: If you've had online interviews, Facebook Live events, videos, or articles etc., embed them on your website. This is an area where your readers can go to watch. It is a great way to promote yourself. You can also post these interviews on Facebook for your readers to enjoy.

6. **BLOG**: Sadly, I don't blog as frequently as I should. There are only so many hours in the day and I have a lot of projects on my plate. But if you do blog, you can set it up on your website so it shows up on Goodreads, your Amazon Author Page, and even Facebook, along with other places you deem helpful.

Goodreads notifies followers every time you post a new blog. This is another form of outreach and engagement. You can blog about anything, but it is important to talk about your writing, particularly when you are working on a new project or are getting ready to launch a new book. That can and will translate into sales. This simple tool allows you to reach and engage readers. My recommendation would be to keep blog posts short and to the point. The longer the post, the more time it takes away from writing.

7. **CONTACT**: Provide a means for readers to reach you through a simple messaging system. This gives readers another avenue to interact, particularly if they have a question. Make time to answer such queries and reply to any comments, even if it is simply a thank you. Don't ever ignore your readers. If you want to make writing a full-time profession, engagement is a must.

8. **SHOP**: I recently added an online shop to my website. This is where readers can go to buy tee shirts, hats, mugs, and bags with artwork related to my books. It is another avenue for engagement. An online shop is very easy to set up, but again, I'd hire a virtual assistant to get the work done and make it easier on yourself.

My agent had been on me for at least a year to get a shop up and running. She told me my readers want more than just books. It turns out she was right. Not only do your readers get something cool to wear, but they proudly walk around advertising your work.

Amazon Author Page/Author Central

Amazon will create an author page specifically for you. I can't tell you how many Indie authors I've run into who are completely unaware of this free service or knew about it but thought it was unimportant. This author page ties directly into your product page and is a must-have because it helps generate sales.

Go to Amazon and search up your favorite author. Pick a book and click on the author's name. You will be taken directly to the author's Amazon page. Besides a listing of the author's blogs and books, there's a nifty little button on that page: Follow. Think of this like a free newsletter service for new book releases. Each time a new book comes out, Amazon sends an email to each reader following the author.

Amazon does not tell you how many people follow you. Forget about asking. Whenever I have a book launch and the new release emails go out, sales spike. If you don't set up an author page, and link your books, you are missing out on sales.

In addition to that, there's very helpful information in Author Central, such as your author rank and access to the NDP BookScan, amongst other things. Check it out.

With each book launch, you must manually add the book to your Author Central page. If you don't, the people following you will not receive an email notification from Amazon that your book just launched. This translates directly into sales.

Facebook Author Page

This is the primary place where I interact with readers. There is a difference between a personal profile and an author page. Your personal page is for you to connect with family and friends, essentially people you know. Your business/author page is for you to talk about your writing, showcase your work, share news, and conduct reader engagement. The author page comes with a ton of additional features.

I'm not going to go through all of the unique bells and whistles Facebook provides for authors, but I will tell you certain strategies for engagement to get your book out to readers and help build your brand.

Not only are you able to post about your writing or what's on your mind, but you can also host Facebook Live events, do polls, giveaways, and share your blog posts while staying connected and interacting with your readers. FB Live is where you go live via a webcam or phone camera and talk about your writing. People who follow you on Facebook will get notified when you go live. They can tune in, watch, and participate by asking questions. That's engagement, and it's vitally important to building your author platform.

The live session is automatically posted to your page when you've finished. I've found most people watch the video after the fact. Facebook Live allows you to communicate directly to your readers, without having to pay for advertising. This is a very powerful tool. Video seems to be currently preferred by FB & Instagram algorithms over written posts and should get you further reach.

Don't be afraid of going live. There is nothing to it. The first couple times you do it, you will be nervous. That's perfectly normal. After you've gone live a few times, it gets old hat. Be sure to watch your videos afterwards. This way you can begin working to eliminate undesirable behaviors such as stuttering or repeating the same word over and over again.

Think you might stress about going live? Don't. Live sessions are not supposed to be polished like a professional newscaster. That's the entire point. The people watching are tuning in to see you because of your writing. They're not expecting everything to be perfect. They want you to be you. So be you.

Start with short live sessions, perhaps five or ten minutes long. Talk about what you have coming up, such as any new releases or updates on current projects. You are also human and your readers want to learn about you personally. As more and more people become engaged with your writing, you'll have additional people tune in. When somebody joins, ask them to say hello and greet them when they do. Again, engagement is key in building your platform and securing a growing reader base.

Facebook also allows you to advertise by boosting posts and creating advertising campaigns. This is a valuable feature because it enables you to drive new and existing readers directly to your Amazon product pages, your website, your newsletter, or even your Facebook Author Page to generate more follows and likes. This allows you to be flexible with your marketing goals and experiment with different approaches.

There's a lot of functionality on the author page and you need to learn about it. Tinker around with Facebook to get a good feel for it. There are plenty of articles and videos online that will help you rapidly become a master. Facebook also has some good tools as well. Do your homework; don't wing it.

Facebook works through a system of likes and follows. Pay attention to these. A like translates into a reader clicking the "Like" button for your page. They are showing support for that page and by default will see content from it. That means that when you make a post, it will show up in their newsfeed, which active users browse daily. It gets complicated with follows, because someone can like your page, but unfollow you or, vice versa, they can follow your page without liking it.

Readers will click to follow an author to receive regular updates, which are always subject to Facebook's algorithm.

When you make a post, it shows up in their newsfeed. Gaining a follower is vital, as it can frequently be better than direct advertising. You can easily go online (I encourage you to do so) to read more about likes and follows to better understand them and how the process works.

The most important thing to keep in mind here is engagement and not to worry or stress too much about how many likes and follows you have. As long as you have steady growth, you should be good. That means your author platform is growing. A cautionary note: When posting on Facebook, don't overdo it. Making multiple posts in a single day, day after day, may turn some people off. Make sure that what you share on social media is relevant. You don't want to clog up newsfeeds with junk. Eventually, readers will ignore your posts or simply unfollow you or, worse, Facebook's algorithm will begin filtering out more of your posts. So be careful.

I generally make humorous posts daily, a funny or thought-provoking picture that's not offensive or overly political. I try to avoid politics because it is not part of my brand. Politics tends to get in the way of building a successful author platform. So why introduce it?

Every few days, I will post something in relation to my writing. This approach keeps readers interested, engaged, and looking forward to my posts. So when I have an important post, such as a book launch announcement, more readers are likely to notice the post and click the link to the Amazon product page.

Twitter

I have a love/hate relationship with Twitter. This platform is another way for you to get your message out, engage readers, and potentially build your brand. The problem with Twitter is that there is a lot of junk and spam to compete against. It's hard to capture someone's attention on Twitter and translate that into sales. I have had mixed results with it, but I still have a Twitter account and when I release a book, I make sure to post. There are active readers following me and I always get sales as a result of the post, just not as many as I do from Facebook.

So, yes, I do get engagement from the platform. However, I don't see a lot of return from it. There are authors who have mastered Twitter, swear by it, and have very engaged followings. I'm not one of them.

My recommendation is to open an account on Twitter and play with it a bit. Learn more about the service and what they have to offer. Again, there are plenty of articles online and free videos about making Twitter work for you. Experiment and make an informed decision before ruling the service out as a primary source of engagement. Still, you need to have it. When it comes to social media, I prefer to focus on one platform to build my audience and continuously nurture my followers.

Goodreads

Amazon's Kindle is linked directly to Goodreads. Create an author profile on Goodreads and add your books to that author profile. Very much like Amazon's Author Central, readers can follow you on Goodreads. Whenever you have a book release, followers receive an email notification. In addition, every time you release a blog post and add it to Goodreads, your followers get notified. This is a free avenue for promotion and engagement. Don't pass it up.

Business Cards

You might be asking yourself, "Why do I need these?" When someone finds out you're an author, it's much easier to hand them a business card and say, simply, "This is me."

Writing is a business. Your professionalism will show as you share your business card to represent yourself. On one side of my business cards I have the covers of my books and on the back the name of the series, a brief blurb, where the book is available, and links to my social media accounts and website. I do not have my email or phone number on my business cards. If they want to reach me, they can do so through Facebook or the contact page on my website.

An easy tip I learned is to leave my business card with the tip every time I go out to eat at a restaurant. If I see a community board, I leave a business card. When I go to a show or convention, I bring them to hand them out to people who are interested in my writing. I also tuck them into promotional books that I give away. Nearly everyone is a potential reader.

Swag/Giveaways

People love free stuff. When I go to shows, I bring bookmarks, mousepads, books, hats, mugs, shirts, and tote bags. I have readers lining up to get them. Sure, it costs hard-earned cash to make them and personal time to give them away, but it's also a business expense. Don't neglect this opportunity. Giveaways help you engage with potential and existing readers.

It's also a way to give something tangible back. A large percentage of my sales are eBook and audiobook, though that is beginning to change as I sell more print books. Most people coming out to see me don't have a physical copy. Giving them a signed book for free is a great way to say thank you for their support. You may also gain a reader for life after a short interaction you have with them. You will likely see them avidly reading your work for years to come.

Giving away swag is another way to build brand and gain lifelong readers. It's also advertising and a business expense. In addition, it never hurts to show your readers you appreciate their support. This is a great way to do that.

Booklinker

The free Booklinker website allows you to create a global link for each book published. Best of all, it's free. Why do you need a global link? There are different Amazon sites for various countries across the globe. If you give somebody in, say, India the US Amazon link to your book, that link will not work for them. They must then go to their specific Amazon and search for your book manually. By providing a global link, they'll be automatically directed to the appropriate Amazon server. Think path of least resistance here. The less effort the prospective reader must go through to find your product, the more likely they will buy.

Newsletter

This is one of the author's most powerful tools for sales generation. Your email newsletter allows you to directly reach your readers without having to advertise or pay for penetration to followers on a platform like Facebook, and unlike social media platforms, you own your email list. This translates into immediate sales on day one of a book launch and helps catapult you up the sales ranks so that other prospective readers see your book and click to buy.

Add a newsletter form on your website in multiple places like your home page and footer. You can post the link to your newsletter or a sign-up button across all your social media platforms. Also, be certain to add a link in your books. Plug it and push it at every opportunity...asking your readers to sign up if they want to receive notifications when new books are released. Over time, your newsletter will grow, especially as more people become engaged and actively read your work.

Promoting your newsletter is very important, because not every reader will follow you on Amazon or social media. The last thing you want to have happen is to lose hard-gained readers in between books for lack of a way to reach them.

I make a point of sending out a newsletter at least every two months. I do this because I don't want to be perceived as spam. If that happens, people will begin unsubscribing. I don't, under any circumstances, want that to happen!

When I send out a newsletter, it's either because I have an update about my writing or I've just released a new book. I try to keep my newsletters as short as possible so the important information I'm attempting to convey is easily read and digested. I also add links to my books and include cover/concept art. I prefer not to overdo it. I also share links to my new blog posts on my social media platforms to keep my followers up to date.

If you are an avid blogger, I recommend you create two different style forms to capture leads from visitors. One form can be for all types of updates, including blog posts and new book releases, and another form just for book releases and writing updates. This way, those readers who only want to learn about new books won't be notified each time you create a new blog post and your open and conversion rates will remain high. This is easily done using tags via your email marketing platform, like MailChimp or ConvertKit.

Your web developer or virtual assistant can help you create different forms, add necessary tags, embed them into your website, and set up automatic broadcasts to optimize your list and simplify your life. Newsletters, social media, and blogging are great ways for your readers to get to know you, like you, and trust you.

Hook Books

I am big believer in giving away books, specifically hook books, that entice new readers into trying my work. Hook books are critical to building your brand. I currently have three series: Chronicles of an Imperial Legionary Officer, The Karus Saga, and Tales of the Seventh. Book one in each of these series is a hook book. By giving them away at book shows, conventions, etc., they are meant to hook the prospect into reading the rest of the series.

At DragonCon this past year, I brought over a thousand books and happily gave them away. Before the convention was over, I had new readers messaging or seeking me out to tell me that they'd already finished reading book one and were excited to dive into book two. This blew my mind, because they were going to the convention to enjoy the show and instead spent precious time reading my book. WOW, how awesome is that?

I have had people leave reviews that they received a free copy of one of my books at a convention or event and loved it. The truth is, people love free stuff. What I find shocking is that at every convention or show, I am usually the only author giving away free books. Don't be afraid of trying it. Set funds aside for giveaways in your marketing budget and plan ahead. Be warned, though, it's exhausting giving away free books, probably more so than selling them. It is also a business expense and a write off.

Links

In your books, you should have links to your website, social media accounts, and newsletter sign up. I also list my books and series, complete with the links to the Amazon product pages. This allows readers to easily find the next book with a click of the link directly from their eBook. A lot of Indie authors fail to do this, and I am convinced it costs them sales.

When the reader finishes one of my books and wants to move on to the next, a link should be waiting to bring them to it or, if they're caught up, to try another of my books in a different series. Links are important and will see the generation of additional sales by anticipating their next move and simplifying the sales process

Exciting/Quality Book Cover

Ever heard someone say, "Don't judge a book by its cover?"

Well, prospective readers without a doubt judge books by their covers. It's not fair, but that's just how it is. Combine an awesome cover with an exciting product description and you increase the chances of converting a prospect into a sale and a potential reader for life. Many Indie authors don't realize this and try to save money on their book covers. You shouldn't. The result is always the same: a poor jacket. This is a mistake of colossal proportions.

When browsing books on Amazon, the prospective reader is shown book covers along with ratings and reviews. Click on a cover and Amazon brings you to the product page to learn more. If you have a captivating cover, you will get more clicks from prospective buyers, and that translates directly into sales. It is that simple.

I can't stress enough how important it is to have an awesome cover. That means your cover art must stand out above the rest, draw the eye, and entice someone to click on your book to learn more. If you're writing in a specific genre, whether it's mystery, crime, science fiction, or fantasy, go to Amazon and check out the covers of the top-selling books in your category. Doing so will show you the standard you must meet and exceed to attract more buyers. You need to have a cover that looks just as good as those bestsellers.

A book with a great cover stands out and catches the eye but, more importantly, convinces prospects to click to its product page to learn more. Think of looking at book covers like window shopping, give online browsers a peek at what is inside your book to capture their imagination.

How can an author get good cover art at an affordable price?

I am going to introduce you to a wonderful website called DeviantArt.

https://www.deviantart.com/

This is a place where artists come together to share their work. Browse and find an artist whose work speaks to you. There are literally hundreds of thousands of artists who've posted their work. The website allows you to private message the artists directly. It is an opportunity to open a conversation about leasing their work or commissioning cover art to be made specifically and exclusively for you.

I found my illustrator on DeviantArt. He does an amazing job at bringing my vision to life. Not only have I commissioned him to create my cover art, but also for concept art to share with my readers. Concept art can help you capture the imagination and build excitement for upcoming projects.

I've even included art inside the books themselves to help readers visualize certain scenes along with custom maps to help the reader get more into the story. I post artwork on my website, Facebook, and Twitter to create excitement and engagement.

When it comes to the cover, don't skimp or try to save a few bucks. Instead, settle for the best. In this digital world you have access to the World Wide Web. Use it. If you don't find the perfect illustrator on DeviantArt... look elsewhere and get the job done right.

Once you have your cover art, a designer will need to set it in the correct dimensions and add the title/text. This is also where book and series branding become important. Try to use similar art, colors, and fonts to solidify your brand identity.

The essentials are just that—tools every author needs to help build his/her author platform and personal brand through the "know, like, and trust" factor.

> RECAP: There are certain essentials every author needs for marketing success.
>
> 1. Author website
> 2. Amazon Author Page
> 3. Author Central
> 4. Facebook Author Page
> 5. Instagram
> 6. Twitter
> 7. Goodreads
> 8. Business cards
> 9. Swag/giveaways
> 10. Booklinker
> 11. Newsletter
> 12. Hook books
> 13. Book links
> 14. Exciting book covers

Chapter Six

Book Marketing • Building a Successful Marketing Plan • Marketing Tools • Marketing Outlets

Bottom Line: If you market it, they will come... and hopefully buy.

Marketing is an important component to publishing your book. It is an area that many Indie authors simply don't understand or ignore until it's too late, usually after their book launch when sales have begun to slow down. To be successful in this publishing environment, you need to understand marketing and apply it.

Don't assume that after you've published your book, your job is done. This is a business, specifically your business. You are the Chief Executive Officer. Your job is not just to write, but also to actively build your brand and grow your audience. The only way to do this is by marketing, and believe me, you can do this. Remember, if I can do it, so can others.

What is marketing?
Simply put, it's identifying prospective readers, promoting your product to them, and converting such prospects directly into sales. Marketing includes research, testing, and analysis. This last bit is critical to being successful. That

means studying the results of your marketing campaigns and drawing conclusions in order to create more effective marketing campaigns and sell more books.

So, let's dig into marketing a bit, shall we?

A comprehensive strategy to attack the market is a must. You can't assume that simply taking out random ads on Amazon or Goodreads will get you what you need to break out from the pack. No single approach to marketing works best. There's no secret ingredient to making one rich and famous. A wide-ranging approach to spreading the word is in order, meaning you need to take action on multiple fronts.

Your focus when it comes to marketing should be essentially growing your reader base/audience. That means you are selling yourself, as the author and personality. You are the brand, the spokesperson, the influencer, and your books are the products you promote. I know some people are not comfortable with self-promotion, but I assure you it is a must as an Indie author.

I believe each author's marketing plan should be tailored specifically to their own writing and reader base. What might work for my books may not work for others. I write in the Fantasy/Science Fiction space and a unique subcategory at that: Greco-Roman Myth & Legend Fantasy.

I am going to provide you with my general thoughts and approach towards book marketing and share several examples of how I market my own books. This should help you develop your own marketing plan for your first book launch as well as help you create an ongoing book marketing strategy.

There are four steps to building a successful marketing plan:

Step One: Identify your target audience.
Step Two: Develop a plan of action and conduct outreach.
Step Three: Analyze campaign data.
Step Four: Rinse and repeat. Repeat steps 1–3 often.

STEP ONE: Identify your target audience. These are the readers you hope will buy your books. The most important part here is researching and understanding your genre. Your target audience should be people who read that genre.

If you're writing Arthurian fiction, you don't want to target readers who are into murder mysteries. When going after a market segment (readers), the narrower your target audience focus, the more sales you will achieve/convert. Meaning that if you reach out to readers who regularly read Arthurian fiction, you will likely see a greater sales conversion rate in relation to prospects than you would by targeting murder mystery readers. Make sense?

If you are able, try to break down the demographics to further define your audience. The narrower your target focus, the easier it is to market to your audience. As an example: If your genre is young adults, there are specific things to consider: What age groups are you writing for? What gender will your book better appeal to? Etc.

STEP TWO: Develop a plan of action and conduct outreach. Once you've identified your target audience and market segment, the next step is figuring out how to reach those readers and develop a plan of action. The good news here is that there are multiple ways to connect with prospective readers. In today's digital world, the main place to find your readers will be online via social media, targeted advertising, and email, just to name a few.

In relation to online marketing, there is paid and organic marketing, which includes social media. Paid advertising is just what it sounds like. The author pays a service to perform marketing functions and help spread the word. Organic advertising can be achieved utilizing social media, bloggers, word of mouth, podcasts, and book reviewers, amongst other avenues, to help you spread the word about your books without paying them to advertise.

As much of this book is Amazon-centric in its focus, I am going to assume you are publishing with Amazon and or enrolled in the KDP Select Program. Through the Kindle Direct Publishing website, you are given the opportunity to promote your book every 90 days. You can run a KDP Select free book promotion or you can discount your book for a short period of time by running a Kindle Countdown Deal. These are powerful tools that allow you to build marketing campaigns around them, using both paid and organic marketing strategies. If you are not enrolled in KDP Select, I urge you to consider it.

As I type this, I can hear some of you say.

"Why the hell would I give away my book for free or at a discount?"

"Dammit, I worked hard on this book and now he wants me to give it away for free? What is he thinking? By gum, readers should pay for it."

Well, the short answer is yes, the readers should pay for your hard work. The long answer is more complicated. If you want to achieve success as an author, you must be primarily focused on building your author platform. This is a forward-thinking, big picture approach, the long-term view. Always keep your goals and brand in mind.

To achieve being a successful full-time author, you must continuously make efforts to reach a wider audience. Running promotions through KDP, such as Kindle Countdown Deals or Giveaways, is a great way to do that. With every single promotion, my audience grows.

Building a self-sustaining reader base does not happen overnight. It takes time and effort. The more people who read and enjoy one of your books, the more readers you will have for successive books. It's really very simple, and there are all sorts of marketing services and tools available to you that help you spread the word when running a promotion.

Remember hook books? This is where they come in especially handy. Amazon's KDP promotions are geared to help you build readership. Heck, Amazon wants you to sell more books. If you do, they make money. However, Amazon is not going to do all the work for you. There is some heavy lifting all Indies must do for themselves.

As I said, your marketing approach should be a comprehensive marketing approach. Having a plan makes it much easier to build your audience. Keep in mind you're not likely to become an overnight success when it comes to publishing. Don't think that you're going to publish your first book and on that day you will retire or quit your job. It just isn't going to happen.

Successfully building your audience takes work, lots of effort, and time. It may also take several books for you to grow a dedicated following capable of supporting you as a full-time author. That's okay. That's how most businesses work. Just be prepared for everything to take time, effort, and energy. Try not to let it frustrate you.

<u>STEP THREE</u>: Review and analyze campaign data. Every time you run a promotion and build an advertising campaign, study the results. There are some basic questions to ask. How many books were sold? How many given away? Dependent upon the type of advertising, there might be additional data to look at, such as Average Cost of Sale (ACOS), Average Price Per Click (APC), how many people were shown specific ads (impressions)... the list goes on. How effective were your keywords? Which keywords performed best?

Always, always study the results. Question your overall strategy and measure against your goals. This allows you to see what is working, what areas need improvement, and where/how to shift your budget. Draw the inferences and conclusions you are able to and adjust your marketing plan accordingly for future promotions.

STEP FOUR: Rinse and repeat. Repeat steps 1-3 as often as you can. Try to improve reach and conversion rates (turning a prospect into a sale) with each new promotion. The larger your audience, the greater your sales will be with each new book release. Remember to continue to build on the "like, know, trust" factor throughout your campaigns to keep your audience engaged and happy.

Promotions

Let's talk about some of the paid and free online tools available to help you get the word out about your books. Any type of outreach provides new readers a chance to learn about your writing.

When sales slow down after an initial launch, my recommendation is to focus exclusively on building your brand and growing your audience leading up to the publication of your next book. Run promotions with an intense focus on expanding your reader base.

Consider using the first book in a series as a hook book. Note: You don't need a series to have a hook book. Choose a book to become your promotional marketing piece. Make sure it's a good one. Think of it as the go-to book to hook new readers on your writing.

Give it away for free or at a discount. Personally, I prefer to make my hook books free as often as I am able. Other authors I know like to run countdown deals. It all comes down to author preference and what works best for you.

Amazon, remember your book needs to be KDP Select, also helps promote your book when you run a free promotion or a Kindle Countdown Deal. This is something not to be taken lightly. Couple that with marketing ads you purchase, and you can easily grow your audience and author platform in leaps and bounds.

My only caution here is to advise against making your book free for more than two or three days at a time. The longer the book is free, the more Amazon's algorithm seems to work against you and the fewer books you will give away on a per day basis. There is also the consideration that when your book returns to regular price, you have a steeper mountain to climb back up the rankings.

I believe there is a perceived value or urgency when you run a sale or free giveaway for a limited period of time, as the reader gets a deal or steal on a popular book. When it comes to perma-free books, some readers think the author is desperate or that they feel compelled to give the book away just to get people to read it. They might even believe there is something deficient with the author's writing. I've had readers at conventions tell me this.

Perception can be a bitch. You don't ever want readers thinking negatively about your work. Cultivating an image of success and quality is a key rung on the ladder to success.

Amazon Giveaways

In addition to regular promotions, Amazon has an awesome tool that allows you to give away eBooks for free to readers you've never met. This is above and beyond the 90-day promotion. Amazon Giveaways is a helpful tool to create buzz, develop followers, and attract new readers. However, you must pay the full price of each book you give away. Giveaways are handled through a random drawing approach.

A handy tip: When you put your hook book up for a Kindle Countdown Deal, for say $0.99, you can buy 50 copies at $0.99 instead of the full price of your hook book and run an Amazon Promotional Giveaway at a later date using the pre-purchased books and save some money.

Price Setting

Amazon also allows you the freedom to set the price of your book. This is really cool because you can essentially lower the price of your book or raise it to do "unofficial" discounts and perform a little marketing outside of Amazon's promotional services. This is also handy if your book is not enrolled in KDP Select.

Marc's Rule: Keep the price affordable.

When you are considering your overall marketing strategy, you want to pay attention to the price of your eBook. Study the competition. See what's the norm and set your price accordingly. There are a lot of readers out there who can't afford or are unwilling to buy a $5.99 eBook from an author they haven't heard about. They are far more likely to purchase a book priced at $3.99 to take a chance on a new author. Think on it. If your book is too expensive, it won't sell or may sell poorly, and that hurts your brand/author platform.

While considering each piece of the puzzle, keep in mind that you need to shamelessly promote yourself. It's a good thing there are plenty of ways for you to do that.

Marketing Services
Book Blogs
Bloggers are a great way to spread the word. Perform a Google search for book blogs in your genre. You can easily find blogs that review books. Don't be shy, reach out. Ask if they might be interested in reviewing your book. If you don't ask, you will never know. The worst they can do is say no.

One blogger giving a good review could translate into hundreds, possibly thousands of new readers. Some blogs do written interviews. If one suggests an interview, take them up on their offer. That's free advertising.

Note: There are bloggers that charge to promote you. Some of the fees can be quite hefty. I would advise staying away from them, as I have not found a good return. That is, unless the blogger has a large and active following or it's a reputable blog tour, then it might make sense to engage their services.

Do your homework; look at their posts. Is there reader engagement in the comment sections of each blog? Do they have a newsletter? Does the blog show up in prospective readers' inboxes? How many users are signed up to their blog? These are all things to consider and can make the difference between a successful promotion and wasted money.

Review Sites
There are a number of websites that do book reviews. These are like book blogs but typically focus almost exclusively on reviews. These sites can be helpful in spreading the word.

A good number of review sites will not consider Indie submissions. Why is that? Because there are a lot of inferior books written by Indies. Basically, reviewers got tired of looking at substandard submissions. Also, reviewers don't enjoy giving poor reviews. They like recommending good books to their readers. This is another reason to get your book in the best shape possible before you launch your book. Get enough reviews and even review sites that normally turn their noses up at Indies will happily review your book.

Be cautious, some review sites charge. I've seen more than a few over the years that promise all kinds of success or guarantee hundreds of reviews or some such nonsense. I have yet to meet a fellow author who has had any luck with these types of promises, particularly the ones that charge a fee.

They may get the promised reviews but have been unable to translate that into any measurable success. Your goal should be focused towards reader engagement. If readers genuinely like your book, they are going to leave reviews, and usually positive ones, too. So why bother paying for reviews? Still, that said, do your homework.

There is always an exception to the rule. You might find a book review service that works well for you, but be cautious. I've heard that Amazon and other platforms do not like any kind of paid reviews.

Online Book Marketing Sites

There are lots of book marketing sites out there to help the self-published author. These should be your bread and butter for book marketing. Such businesses range in services provided and price.

My favorite marketing sites to use are always those that market through newsletters, where a prospective reader gets an email about my book. Take advantage of these services. They help you boost your reach when it comes to KDP Select promotions or new book launches.

Facebook

Do not neglect Facebook. I am going to repeat myself a little for those who skipped ahead to this chapter. Create a Facebook Author Page. This is different than your personal profile. Your business page is where readers will come to connect with you. It is also a great outlet to get out the latest news on your writing, advertise, and share promotional information, artwork, funny stories, whatever.

Facebook is where I have the most engagement with my readers. Readers can message you directly on Facebook. Make sure you download the Facebook business tools available to you to stay connected with your readers, track promotions, and review analytics. Do not ignore your audience. This is an opportunity for you to spend a few minutes of your time and convert a reader or prospect to a devoted follower for life.

If a reader posts on your page, or comments on one of your posts that they loved your book, don't be shy. Thank them for their kind words and ask them if they wouldn't mind leaving you a review on Amazon or Goodreads. Don't be afraid to ask for reviews. Usually if you do, the reader will leave one, and it will generally be fair. Amazon's algorithm is keyed to respond to reviews. The more good reviews you have, the more Amazon promotes your book to similar readers.

You can also conduct advertising campaigns via Facebook to attract new readers, not only to your Facebook Author Page, but also directly to Amazon to purchase your book. This is great when you are running a promotion. There is a lot of functionality with Facebook ads.

That said, Facebook advertising is a hard nut to crack. It's difficult to translate dollars spent and clicks into actual sales. Most authors struggle to see any kind of success. It takes a good deal of personal experimentation to learn what works for your audience and for specific reader demographics.

Facebook, like Amazon and Google Ads, allows you to drill down, targeting specific regions, demographics, and interests by utilizing keywords. It is a phenomenal tool but, again, should be one of many components of your overall marketing plan.

Twitter

This is another tool you can use to help spread the word. The downside with Twitter is there's a lot of junk content, so it's more difficult to penetrate the crap to get to actual readers. I spent a great deal of time experimenting with Twitter and had only mixed results to show for my efforts and dollars. That doesn't mean that you ignore Twitter—just the opposite.

As your brand grows, active readers will follow you. But a word of caution: If you have ten thousand people following you, that does not translate into ten thousand readers. The same goes for Facebook or any other social media platform.

My experience with Twitter is that you will see a much smaller number of people actively reading your work, engaging, and interacting than you would get on Facebook. There are authors out there who love Twitter. They've been able to get it to work successfully for them. I have not.

Experiment for yourself to determine whether or not the platform will be useful for you. There are a number of tools Twitter has online to help market yourself, including the ability to run advertisements. There are a plethora of online articles and videos on YouTube to help you get a better understanding of how you can perform marketing via Twitter.

Instagram
Instagram is another social media platform I plan on experimenting with more this year. It is on my long list of things to do. There are authors who have had great success with this platform.

More importantly, Instagram is owned and tied in directly with Facebook advertising, and you can run your promotions on two separate platforms and track performance and analytics all from one place. Pretty handy, huh?

Amazon & Google, SEO
These two websites are monster marketing machines and should be part of your overall comprehensive marketing plan.

Does the thought of working with these monsters scare you? It shouldn't. There are plenty of free articles and YouTube videos on how to use Amazon and Google advertising effectively. Tons of books have been written as well. Do a little homework before you begin using these tools. That way, there is less chance of wasting your money and a better opportunity to maximize your potential reach.

As with social media advertising, Amazon and Google provide you with the ability to target specific demographics in a detailed and comprehensive manner.

Amazon's direct advantage is that, through their marketing services, authors can advertise directly to readers on the Kindle platform and on Amazon websites as well. This is incredibly powerful, as this is the number one place eBook readers visit to find new books. Somewhere around 80% of all eBook sales happen through Amazon. That is a staggering figure. Authors using Amazon's marketing and advertising have an edge since their services are exclusive to the Amazon platform.

It's important to note that it is very hard to map a definitive correlation between advertising and Kindle Unlimited sales. Remember, Kindle Unlimited is Amazon's subscription eBook borrowing program. It is Amazon's virtual library, but not all eBooks subscribe to this platform.

As an author you get paid per page read. Understanding how advertising works with KU is more of an art form. Generally, when your paid advertising campaign on Amazon starts, you will see an increase in page reads. If you don't, your advertising is not as effective as it could be. The more advertising you do on Amazon, the more you will understand how it works and this will allow you to customize your marketing and advertising approach.

Creating an advertising campaign through Amazon Marketing Services (AMS) is surprisingly easy. However, it is also complicated. By complicated, I mean it is deep. There is a lot that you need to learn. Do your homework.

There are people out there spending thousands upon thousands of dollars on advertising through the Amazon Marketing Services and Google Ads each month. Do I think you need to spend thousands upon thousands of dollars to move up in the ranks? The short answer is no, I don't. For some authors, spending thousands of dollars works. They have the system down and completely understand how it operates and watch it daily like a hawk. They invest countless hours analyzing and scrutinizing their advertising campaigns.

My ads are generally smaller and more targeted. My overall approach to marketing has always been broader, across many platforms, and not solely based upon AMS or Google Ads. Think of it as proportioned marketing.

As a result of this comprehensive approach, I am able to be very successful at writing, without having to spend crazy amounts of money on advertising. It is an approach I urge you to consider.

Google Ads is very similar to Amazon Marketing Services. However, this service allows your ads to show up on multiple platforms, not just exclusive to Amazon. It is, in my humble opinion, something that you can approach easily. However, like everything else, it may take some time to get the hang of it to the point where it starts making you money.

Google Ads allows you to publish text ads that will show up under search results. Just like Amazon Marketing Services, Google Ads has surprising depth, allowing you to drill down your targeting. This is an important tool that can really help drive traffic to your product page.

Then there is SEO, which stands for Search Engine Optimization. This is designed to help drive organic traffic to a website. There are books, videos, and online classes on how to excel at this marketing approach. I have done very little with SEO. That said, I've heard some authors claim they have had success with it that translated into definable sales. My recommendation would be to look into SEO and determine if it is worth your time.

Any type of online advertising should be approached with a long-term goal in mind. You should create campaigns that last several weeks so that you can evaluate them, not only on a daily basis, but also weekly and monthly. The long-term approach gives you a better understanding of the whole picture to determine what is working for you and what is not. When you are more informed, you can begin experimenting to see if you can improve your marketing results.

Remember, marketing is about refining your approach to advertising to maximize sales. It is the same whether you are advertising on Facebook, Amazon, Google, or similar platforms. Your focus should be set on getting the most bang for your buck to maximize your marketing and advertising budget while expanding your reach and growing your audience.

My advice is to start small and then scale up as you begin learning what works for you and what doesn't. Don't make the mistake of dumping a lot of money into something at the beginning with the hopes that, if you throw enough crap against the wall, something will stick. It almost always doesn't.

I can't guarantee that you will have any significant success in using online marketing. There are so many factors involved, from your ad copy, to your product description, to the quality of your reviews, cover, etc. Remember, any approach to marketing should be a comprehensive one. If you are hoping to simply take out an ad and sell a ton of books, I do not believe you will be very successful.

Don't have a big budget? As I said, start small, spending a few dollars a month, then scale upward as your sales increase and you can support more advertising. You don't need to spend a whole lot of money to make a splash. Building your platform takes time.

When you look at your advertising over the course of the year, those dollars do add up and it can become quite a large expenditure. Advertising and promotional costs are business expenses. Just make sure you work with a tax professional when doing your taxes so that what you claim is legal and you don't get in trouble.

A good rule of thumb is to set your advertising budget at 10–15% of your writing take. This allows you to continue to build your brand and get your book out there to new readers, while at the same time making some money.

As a brand new author, you may want to budget $1,000 to $3,000 for advertising during your book launch. This will give you a little bang to help get the word out and see you off to a good start to building your author platform. You must treat your writing as a serious business, because it is YOUR business. Budgeting is an incredibly important component of any business.

Press

I recommend attacking different mediums to help get the word out. A good way to do that is to write a press release and send it out to the local newspapers, local magazines, or national publications relevant to your genre. Optimally, it is up to you. The same goes for your local news stations. Tell them that you'd be willing to do an interview. Local news outlets love stories about authors in their backyard.

All of this helps you get the word out and generate not only buzz, but sales. Granted, the sales will likely be small, but let's be honest: Every single book sold counts. Each reader who enjoys your book has the potential to become a reader for life. Don't pass this up.

What works for me might not work for you. There are plenty of examples of sample press releases online that you can view for free. Write a good one. Keep it simple, to the point, and straightforward.

Example of a press release used for *The Tiger's Fate*

FOR IMMEDIATE RELEASE

Contact: XXXXXXX
XXXXXXXXXX
XXX-XXX-XXXX
XXXX@XXXXX.com

2017 IPPY Gold Medal Winner for Best Science Fiction, Fantasy & Horror E-Book Independent Publisher Book Awards

Best-Seller The Tiger's Fate (Chronicles of an Imperial Legionary Officer Book 3) Wins Gold IPPY

Florida, May, 2017- Local best-selling author Marc Alan Edelheit's *The Tiger's Fate* takes Gold at this year's Independent Publisher Book Awards. This is Marc's second IPPY; his first was for *Stiger's Tigers (Chronicles of an Imperial Legionary Officer Book 1)* that won Bronze in 2016.

Conducted annually, the Independent Publisher Book Awards honor the year's best independently published titles from around the world. The awards are intended to bring increased recognition to the thousands of exemplary independent, university, and self-published titles published each year. The IPPY is celebrating its 21st year of awards.

In *The Tiger's Fate*, Stiger, his men, and his new dwarven allies have fallen back behind the great walls of Castle Vrell. Stiger finds himself named Legate of the Vanished, the long lost 13th Legion. This title and his own word binds him to the terms of the Compact an ancient and mystical alliance formed nearly two thousand years before.

The snows have come and the mountain summit into Vrell is impassable. On one side of the pass sits an army of the Cyphan Confederacy some twenty thousand strong. On the other side Stiger, his company, the remnants of the 13th Legion and a dwarven army. Each side is waiting for the spring thaw.

Bottled up in the Vrell valley, Stiger and his elven companion, Eli, learn of Garand Thoss, an ancient and abandoned dwarven city. Within its hallowed halls resides a prize of unimaginable value; a prize that will reveal the true history of the empire, and force Stiger to face a new enemy more deadly than he has ever faced before...

"I am extremely humbled to win Gold and would like to thank my fans, agents, editors and beta readers for the success of the series." –Marc Alan Edelheit

For queries regarding the film options or publishing rights for Edelheit's books, please contact Andrea Hurst at ****@****.com

Author: Marc Alan Edelheit has a bachelor's degree in science and obtained a master's in education as a reading and writing specialist. He is currently an executive in the healthcare industry who stays up late at night to work on his novels. Marc has traveled the world from Asia to Europe, even at one point crossing the border at Check Point Charlie in Berlin toward the end of the cold war. Marc is the ultimate history fan and incorporates much of that passion into his work to bring greater realism to his fans. He is also an avid reader, devouring several books a week ranging from history to science fiction and fantasy. Marc currently resides in New Hope, Pennsylvania, just miles from where Washington crossed the Delaware. He is the author of *Stiger's Tigers*, *The Tiger*, and *The Tiger's Fate*. His first book opened the door to a new genre, Military Fiction, which has been performing well and growing daily. Mark can be found attending conventions throughout the year, this year he will be at DragonCon, ComicCon and SuperCon. For more information, visit Marc's website at http://www.macnovels.com/.

The Tiger's Fate
Chronicles of an Imperial Legionary Officer Book 3

Author
Marc Alan Edelheit

Category
Science Fiction
Military Fantasy

Soft Cover
978-1534899025
$11.99

Kindle eBook
$4.99

Availability
Amazon.com

Radio Talk Shows & Podcasts

Reach out to radio talk shows and podcasts that focus on books or entertainment. The worst that they can say is, "No, we're not interested." More likely, they simply won't respond. Again, if you don't ask, you don't get. It's another way to help get the word out and generate buzz, especially if you score an interview.

The best way to land interviews is to hire a publicity/marketing firm and let them arrange it for you. A word of caution: This is pricey. I've never met an author who was 100% satisfied after hiring a firm, but they do score interviews.

During any interview, tell the listeners where they can get your book: "My book is available on Amazon, Kindle Unlimited, Audible, and in print."

YouTube Interviewers & Reviewers
This is another great way to help generate buzz. Search for book reviewers and author interviewers on YouTube and contact them to help you get the word out about your book.

Appearances
Make a splash with personal appearances. Remember, with your first book, you're not Tom Clancy or Brandon Sanderson. You are you, and your focus is brand building. A great place to start is at your local library. Contact them, ask if they have any local author expos, or offer to give a free talk. Generally, I've found that libraries have events throughout the year to support local authors. I've gone to a number of these and they've proven very effective. This is a great place to give your hook books away.

There are also book tradeshows. You can purchase a table at many of these shows or attend as a guest. For most science fiction and fantasy conventions, as an author, you can apply for status as a guest or an attending professional to get in for free. There are typically author panels you may be asked to participate in, and if you're not, seek them out. This is an opportunity for you to get out in front of people who love reading to talk about your writing and, more importantly, promote your brand.

My recommendation is to bring books and swag to give away to help grow your author platform. These types of conventions tend to be hard work and exhausting. I always come home feeling like I need to sleep for a week afterwards.

Offer to speak at local schools, colleges, and universities. Reach out to literature departments and let them know you would love to come in and talk about how you wrote your first book or any particular subject they may be interested in as it relates to your vocation. Writer conferences can also be a great place for new writers, as you have the opportunity to build or join a writing community and potentially get yourself in front of agents.

Local fairs are another creative way to get some attention. You can rent a table or booth, with the ultimate goal of meeting potential readers. I know a number of authors who attend library functions, conventions, book shows, and fairs to sell their books. They come away having sold 30 or 60 books, perhaps even more. When I attend shows, as I've said, I take a different approach. I bring my hook books to give away, along with some swag.

People love free stuff. It's an opportunity for you to spend two or three minutes speaking with somebody about your writing, sharing your love for what you do, and making an impression upon them. Such encounters build excitement and a lasting memory in the reader.

Book Awards

Lastly, there are also book awards. Submit your book or books to award contests. Awards are a great way, if you win, to get immediate attention. Without entering these contests, you will never know if you could have won. Put yourself out there and take a risk.

All of the above suggestions take time, effort, and energy. You don't have to do it all at once. It's like climbing that mountain. Make a plan. Do a little bit at a time. You can also hire a virtual assistant to help you.

Building your author platform as an Indie author in today's marketplace is not a sprint, but a marathon. Don't fall into the trap of believing that your first book will make your career. That's great if it does, but for the rest of us, you want to build your platform and increase your audience steadily with each new release. I continue to do this with each and every new book I write.

Sample Marketing Campaigns

I could write an entire book just on the designing and conducting of effective marketing campaigns. I plan to do just that at some point in the future. But that is not the purpose of this book, which is more of a high-level overview and guide to building your author platform. Still, I would be remiss not to provide examples of how to design a basic marketing campaign.

Keep in mind … this is a *basic* approach to help you get started building a plan customized to meet your own needs. Do not copy what I've provided, but build upon it. I've always felt the most effective campaigns are always those you design and execute yourself.

All marketing plans should be multifaceted, a comprehensive approach to sales, if you will. As such, plans can become detailed and complex. Don't stress. Start with the basics. As you learn, refine your plan, layering in depth and complexity. When you first launch your book, your brand is likely to be nonexistent, meaning prospective readers won't know who you are. It will be your job to build your author platform to gain recognition and in turn grow your author platform.

Remember, breakout hits are the exception and not the rule. Be prepared for years of platform building to get to the point where you can take writing full-time. Every reader gained is one step forward.

When it comes to online advertising, you are primarily looking for clicks to your product page. If you're not getting any, or few, clicks, it is likely that your ad copy and associated picture/cover are not engaging. Ad copy is the text of the ad. Change it up, make it better and more exciting. If you're getting click-throughs but little to no sales, it could be your product description is lacking and not as gripping as it could be.

This means the potential customers were interested enough to follow the ad down the rabbit hole to the product page, but when they got there, the book description was less than compelling. Think about changing it. As I said, marketing can be complex. There is a lot to take in, study, and infer. Everyone has to start at the beginning, with baby steps.

SAMPLE CAMPAIGN #1

FIRST BOOK LAUNCH
Month 1 – Suggested Marketing Budget $1,000 – $3,000

1. Press Releases
2. Organic Social Media Marketing Posts
3. Social Media Advertising Campaign
4. Book Marketing Sites
5. AMS Marketing Campaign
6. Google Ads Marketing Campaign
7. Book Blogs, Book Tours, and Book Reviews
8. YouTube and Podcast Interviews

Press Releases (see sample)
Create a press release to share with local newspapers, regional magazines, relevant publications, and local news outlets. Don't forget to offer to give free interviews and complimentary presentations about topics you are an expert in.

Organic Social Media Marketing Posts
As previously suggested, you should have created your author social media pages to build your brand and author platform many, many months ago. Now that you are somewhat established and have a following, you should start advertising on social media to promote your new book.

Here's what you will do to create hype and build momentum before your new book launch. Create a series of related social media posts about your new book to include engaging posts about your writing and your life as an author on your Facebook Author Page, Instagram, and/or Twitter pages.

Get into the habit of posting regularly. Once or twice per day should be enough. The plan is to post regularly in order to get noticed by the algorithm so that your posts are shown to your followers on a regular basis. Do not overdo it. Quality over quantity will help grow your organic reach over time.

Share pictures, relevant life updates, book artwork, articles of interest to your genre, your blog posts, and book covers amongst other things. Share posts to help readers relate to you, make a connection, and feel compelled to want to create a relationship with you. Again, build on the "know, like, trust" factor.

Social Media Advertising Campaign

Create a campaign composed of several ads through Facebook Ads Manager or on Twitter. Make sure the ad copy you write is not only exciting, but compelling. Include a picture of your cover, yourself, or an image related to your book in the ads to build excitement.

Link the picture in the ad directly to your Amazon product page for prospective readers to click through to learn more about your book and purchase it. Target your desired audience and boost your posts. If you are concerned about the complexity of doing this, read online articles, watch tutorials, or take a free online class to learn more.

I recommend beginning with a low dollar amount budget. Try 2–4 different ads at $5 a day per ad. Run the ads for two weeks and learn which ones get you the best traction and click-through rates. For Facebook and Instagram, this information can be found on Facebook Ads Manager.

Refine and support your advertising according to the analytics that are delivered. Increase your ad budget if you wish to reach more prospective readers and are seeing significant success. These ad buys are helping you get the word out about your book.

Book Marketing Sites
I have listed several book marketing sites in Chapter 7. Some of these are great help at advertising the launch of new books. Go through my list and find marketing sites that support new book launches and engage their services. Make sure you read through the services that are available to determine if it's a good fit for your book before purchasing.

Here are some that I've found success with:
Book Tweeters
Author Ad Network
BookBub Ads—this is an ad you can run for days, weeks, and months to drive traffic to your product page
Kindle Boards (KBoards)
Kindle Daily Nation

AMS & Google Ads/Advertising Campaigns
Using demographic and interest targeting, take out several different ads with varying ad copy and run them over several weeks. Allow your advertising campaigns time to work. Unlike Facebook advertising, sometimes it can take days or even weeks before the campaigns begin showing good results.

You can start with a low dollar spend and ramp up or refine as needed. The idea is to drive traffic to your product page. Carefully study the results. You can experiment to see what works and what does not. Refine as needed and always reinforce success.

Book Blogs, Book Tours, Podcasts & Book Reviews

Do a search for related blogs, book tours, podcasts, and book reviewers in the genre you are writing. Reach out and see if they are interested in reviewing your book, including your book in their book tour, and/or interviewing you on their blog or podcast.

In my experience, the free ones seem to deliver more success at helping you get the word out. Plan ahead and reach out early on so that you can line up several different types of marketing efforts leading up to your book launch. See my notes about this in Chapter 7.

YouTube Interviews

Search for YouTubers who specialize in reviewing books in your selected genre. Reach out and offer to do an interview. Interviews are a fun and easy way to help you spread the word about your new book and can easily translate into sales.

SAMPLE CAMPAIGN #2

SUBSEQUENT BOOK LAUNCH
Suggested Monthly Marketing Budget $1,000 – $3,000

1. Organic Social Media Marketing Posts
2. Newsletter Release
3. Press Releases
4. Social Media Advertising Campaign
5. Book Marketing Sites
6. AMS Marketing Campaign
7. Google Ads Marketing Campaign
8. Book Blogs, Book Tours, and Book Reviews
9. YouTube and Podcast Interviews
10. Early Review Copies to Fans
11. Cover Reveals

Organic Social Media Marketing Posts
Begin months in advance with a social media campaign, utilizing Facebook, Twitter, and Instagram. Build up excitement amongst your followers by posting updates, concept art, excerpts from your books, contests, etc.

Basically, you want to do anything that will generate interest and keep your readers engaged and actively following your posts. If you succeed, when it comes time for the book launch, more people should be paying attention to what you are doing.

As previously suggested, you should have created your author social media pages to build your brand and author platform many, many months ago. Now that you are somewhat established and have a following, you should start advertising on social media to promote your new book targeting prospective new readers.

Here's what you will do to build hype and momentum before your new book launch. Create a series of related social media posts about your new book to include engaging posts about your writing and your life as an author on your Facebook Author Page, Instagram, and/or Twitter pages.

Get into the habit of posting regularly. Once or twice per day should be enough. The plan is to post regularly in order to get noticed by the algorithm so that your posts are shown to your followers on a regular basis. Do not overdo it. Quality over quantity will help grow your organic reach over time.

Share pictures, relevant life updates, book artwork, articles of interest to your genre, your blog posts, and book covers amongst other things. Share posts to help readers relate to you, make a connection, and feel compelled to want to create a relationship with you. Again, build on the "know, like, trust" factor.

Newsletter Release

When your book launches, send out a newsletter blast. Make sure you include a universal link to the product page using Booklinker. This should immediately get you moving up in the bestseller ranks as the people signed up to your newsletter begin purchasing your book.

The more visible you are to other prospective readers in the ranking, the greater the opportunity for additional purchases. Get enough activity and Amazon may even give your new book the #1 New Release tag for the month, which is always nice and can help you generate sales.

Press Releases

Create a press release for your new book to share with local newspapers, regional magazines, relevant publications, and local news outlets. Don't forget to offer to give free interviews and complimentary presentations about topics you are an expert in.

Social Media Advertising Campaign

Create a campaign composed of several ads through Facebook Ads Manager and/or on Twitter for both the preceding books and new book. Make sure your ad copy is exciting and compelling. Always include a picture of your cover, yourself, or an image related to your book in the ads to build excitement.

Link the picture in the ad directly to your Amazon product page for prospective readers to click through to learn more about your book and purchase it. Target your desired audience and boost your posts. If you are concerned about the complexity of doing this, read online articles, watch tutorials, or take a free online class to learn more.

I recommend beginning with a low dollar amount budget. Try 2–4 different ads. $2–$5 a day per ad may be a reasonable social media campaign budget if your marketing budget allows. Run the ads over the course of 1–2 weeks. Determine which ones work best. Refine and support the advertising that is showing success.

Book Marketing Sites

With a subsequent book launch you can choose to go large or stick to a budget. I would recommend staying with a budget to promote subsequent book launches. Amazon Free Book Promotions and Kindle Countdown Deals (KDP Select) seem to deliver the most bang for your buck at this stage. They can easily help you rise in the ranks where you acquire additional readers.

My recommendation would be to tie a book launch into an Amazon Free Book Promotion or a Kindle Countdown Deal for an existing book or books and use the book marketing sites for the promotion to allow you to get a bigger bang for your buck.

Author Ad Network
BookBub Ads—this is an ad you can run for days, weeks, and months to drive traffic to your product page.
BookGorilla
eBookHounds
FK Books and Tips
The Fussy Librarian
Book Tweeters
KindleBoards (KBoards)
Kindle Daily Nation
Robin Reads

AMS & Google Ads/Advertising Campaigns

As with your initial book launch campaign, keep your focus on targeting specific demographics and interests. Start with a low dollar amount and run the ads over several weeks.

Be patient. Unlike social media marketing, which can produce results rather quickly, this type of campaign can take several days or even weeks before you can see measurable results.

Carefully study and analyze your data to find out what works and what doesn't and use it to further refine your paid advertising campaign. Always reinforce success.

I would recommend buying ads on both your new book and any existing books to see which ads gain better traction. You will be able to track performance of your ads very easily using the Google Ads and Amazon's built-in reporting packages.

Book Blogs, Book Tours, Podcasts & Book Reviews
Do a search for related blogs, book tours, podcasts, and book reviewers in the genre you are writing. Reach out and see if they are interested in reviewing your book, including your book in their book tour, and/or interviewing you on their blog or podcast.

In my experience, the free ones seem to deliver more success at helping you get the word out. Plan ahead and reach out early on so that you can line up several different types of marketing efforts leading up to your book launch. See my notes about this in Chapter 7.

YouTube Interviews
Search for YouTubers who specialize in reviewing books in your selected genre. Reach out and offer to do an interview. Interviews are a fun and easy way to help you spread the word about your new book and can easily translate into sales.

SAMPLE CAMPAIGN #3

IN BETWEEN BOOKS – MAJOR PROMOTIONS AND CONTINUOUS ADVERTISING
Suggested Monthly Marketing Budget $1,000+

1. Promotional Campaigns
2. Organic Social Media Marketing Posts
3. Giveaway Promotions
4. Book Marketing Sites
5. Award Contests
6. Social Advertising Campaign
7. AMS Marketing Campaign
8. Google Ads Marketing Campaign

Promotional Campaigns

With Amazon you can run a free promotion or Kindle Countdown Deal every 90 days if your book is enrolled in KDP Select. This is very useful and one of the primary tools I recommend for the Indie author to grow their brand and reach. Don't underestimate the importance of these promotions. As I say elsewhere, Amazon's built-in promotions should be your bread and butter. They can easily help you rise in the ranks where you acquire additional readers.

Run free Kindle promotions or countdown deals at every available opportunity for your hook books. Support the promotions with direct advertising with book marketing sites, AMS & Google Ads ads, Twitter, Instagram, and Facebook.

Promotions: This is where you can really rock at building your brand and increasing your audience. It's an opportunity to grow your reader base by leaps and bounds using the springboard that is Amazon's built-in promotions: Free Giveaways and Kindle Countdown Deals.

Continual Advertising: Steady growth should also be a goal. Outside of promotions, it's also smart to have continuous advertising working in your favor to draw prospective readers to your product page.

Note: If Amazon ever offers you a Kindle Daily Deal, Monthly Promotion, or Prime Reading option, my recommendation is to take it and then promote the heck out of it when the Amazon promotion kicks in.

These types of Amazon offers really help grow your audience and are very special because Amazon is working overtime on your behalf. Never pass on an Amazon promotion. They know what they are doing and you should work double time to advertise your Amazon promotions whenever possible. Take my word for it.

Organic Social Media Marketing Posts

Conduct an ongoing organic social media campaign utilizing the Facebook, Twitter, and Instagram platforms. Continue to engage and build excitement amongst your followers to build on the "know, like, trust" factor we discuss in this book.

Giveaway Promotions

Continual: This is where hook books come in handy. Give away signed copies of your books as part of online contests with your readers. Make personal appearances and give books away as opposed to selling them. Utilize Amazon

Giveaways to hold contests to drive readers to follow you and read your books.

Book Marketing Sites

Promotions: You have a choice here. You can go small or large, spending a few hundred to several thousand dollars. It all depends on your budget and desired reach. See Chapter 7 for a long list of book marketing sites. Pick the ones you feel are right for your book.

Award Contests

Enter award contests whenever possible. Join their newsletters to be notified when contest submissions open and new contests are added. See notes and lists of websites on Chapter 7.

Social Media Advertising Campaigns

Promotions: Create several advertisements using Facebook's Ad Manager and/or Twitter for both your preceding books and your new book. Make sure the ad copy is exciting. Include a picture of your book cover or art. Link the picture on the advertisement directly to your Amazon product page for prospective readers to click through and purchase. Target your desired audience and boost your sales.

I would recommend two ads with a pop, at a minimum of $50 a day per ad, until the promotion is over. This is the best time to increase your advertising budget. Make Amazon's promotions work in your favor.

Continual Advertising in Addition to Promotions: Allow successful ads to run on a continuous basis to generate steady sales and increase your reader base and author platform. Scale up if you wish to reach more prospective readers.

Revisit your budget and marketing campaign often, with an eye toward refining your approach to boost sales.

AMS/Google Ads Buys
Continual: Once again, using demographic and interest targeting, along with everything else you learned through your prior campaigns, take out several different ads, with varying ad copy and images. Run these ads over a few weeks. You can start low dollar and ramp up. The primary idea here is to drive consistent traffic to the Amazon product pages for your books.

Typically, these types of ad campaigns are geared towards generating continued interest by driving prospective readers to your product pages day after day. Such campaigns should generate steady, consistent sales over an extended period of time and make your books more visible on Amazon's category-specific bestseller rankings, thereby generating additional sales.

With each sale, you have the potential to add a reader for life, making any subsequent launches more successful. Your new books should climb the rankings faster and stay there longer. This generates additional purchases from visibility alone.

RECAP: There is no one magic bullet to marketing. No one service will make you successful. You must reach consumers via several platforms at the same time.

1. Marketing efforts should be focused on a more comprehensive approach/overall strategy with the focus of increasing reader base.
2. Identify your target audience, develop a plan of action, and conduct outreach. Analyze campaign data, refine your approach, and repeat.
3. Utilize all of the tools at your disposal: promotions, giveaways, price adjustments, book blogs, review sites, book marketing sites, Facebook, Twitter, Instagram, Amazon, Google marketing, the press, radio talk shows, podcasts, YouTube interviews, book reviewers, appearances, book awards, etc.

Sample Templates

I have included sample templates to help you become more organized and successful at planning during the book writing and launch process. You can visit my website, print or download these templates and use them as they are or you can customize them to create your own personalized worksheets.

As an entrepreneur, it is important to create and follow your story outline and marketing campaign while staying on budget. I hope you find these templates useful for planning your storyline and planning future book launches. https://www.maenovels.com/

BOOK BUDGET

BOOK EXPENSES	ESTIMATED BUDGET
Developmental Editor	$
Copy Editor	$
Proofreader	$
Cover Design	$
Formatting, Layout, and Interior Design	$
Book Launch Marketing	$
Continuous Marketing	$
Other	$
Other	$
Other	$
TOTAL ESTIMATED BUDGET	$

MARKETING BUDGET

Suggested Monthly Marketing Budget $1,000 – $3,000
PROMOTION DATES: _____

ADVERTISING CAMPAIGN	ESTIMATED BUDGET
Press Releases	Free
Organic Social Media Marketing Posts	Free
Facebook Advertising Campaign	$
Instagram Advertising Campaign	$
Twitter Advertising Campaign	$
Book Marketing Site 1	$
Book Marketing Site 2	$
Book Marketing Site 3	$
AMS Advertising Campaign	$
Google Ads Advertising Campaign	$
Book Blogs, Book Tours, and Book Reviews	Free
YouTube and Podcast Interviews	Free
TOTAL ESTIMATED BUDGET	$

MARKETING CAMPAIGN

PROMOTION DATES: _____

MARKETING CAMPAIGN NAME	SCHEDULED DATES
Press Release 1:	
Press Release 2:	
Press Release 3:	
Facebook Ad 1:	
Facebook Ad 2:	
Instagram Ad 1:	
Instagram Ad 2:	
Twitter Ad 1:	
Twitter Ad 2:	
Book Marketing Site 1:	
Book Marketing Site 2:	
Book Marketing Site 3:	
AMS Campaign:	
Google Ads Campaign:	
Book Blog 1:	
Book Blog 2:	
Book Blog 3:	
Book Tour 1:	
Book Tour 2:	
Book Review Site 1:	
Book Review Site 2:	
Book Review Site 3:	
YouTube Interview 1:	
YouTube Interview 2:	
Podcast Interview 1:	
Podcast Interview 2:	
Podcast Interview 3:	

BOOK OUTLINE

CHAPTER #: _____

CHARACTERS: _____
_____
_____

TIME OF DAY: _____

WEATHER: _____

SETTING: _____
_____
_____

OBJECTIVE: _____
_____

SUMMARY: _____
_____
_____
_____
_____
_____

Chapter Seven

Important Lists: Most Everything an Author
Needs to Build Brand & Sell Books

Bottom Line: Start making lists of everything you've done and plan on doing to build your author platform.

Marc's Rule: Become as organized as possible.

The companies and services listed below are easily searchable on the web. However, the internet is the Wild West and for someone looking to publish their first book it can be quite overwhelming. Still, even for established authors it's a lot of work. You just don't know who to work with or what type of services you may need.

I wrote this book to help you navigate the ocean that is the publishing industry with an eye to helping you make a splash in this heavily saturated marketplace. I am sharing with you everything I wish I would've known before I self-published my first book.

I have done some of the legwork for you and compiled a lengthy list of entities offering self-publishing services. This is by no means a comprehensive list. But it is a great place for you to begin. If you don't find what you are looking for below, then the internet awaits.

Cautionary note: There are bad actors out there. They have professional websites and fantastic pitches that sometimes promise you the world. I myself have been duped and taken for a ride on more than one occasion. I found the experience painful. Always research an entity before you engage their services.

Ask for references and check their reviews. Also request samples of their work. If they refuse to provide you with any of this, run and don't look back. A professional entity should be more than willing to provide references, recommendations, and examples of their work. They want your business. By doing simple checks like this, you can limit the chances of making a mistake and getting into bed with a bad actor.

I have done my best to list companies and services with good reputations. That does not mean, by choosing to work with any of those listed below, you won't have problems, headaches, or become dissatisfied with their work. Most likely, you will have a good experience, but I simply can't guarantee that you will. As usual in any line of work, please proceed with caution and at your own risk.

IMPORTANT: READ THIS!
Self-Publishing Advice from the Alliance of Independent Authors:

This website is a must-visit and a good resource for any Indie author looking to publish their first novel or one hundredth novel. These people monitor the self-publishing industry and do their best to rate companies and services by feedback from users. It's kind of like the Better Business Bureau for the Indie publishing industry.

Some of the information may be out of date, but much of it is still fairly good. If you are thinking about working with a company, whether it's for marketing, publishing, etc., this website should be your first stop to check how they stack up. Handy, huh? If you have a bad experience, I would encourage you to report it to them as well.

SWFA Writer Beware Page
Hosted by the Science Fiction and Fantasy Writers of America, this site is also a must stop. They provide alerts (watchdog kind of stuff), heads-up on a wide range of issues, and tons of very handy information. Spend some time looking it over.

Independent Book Publishers Association
This is another good group. They are a nonprofit, with part of their focus directly on Indie authors. Spending some time on their website might prove quite helpful. Make sure to check out their membership benefits. Members get serious discounts when it comes to publishing-related services.

Association of Authors' Representatives
This organization pretty much sets the standard for agent quality. Each agent must meet a certain level of experience and agree to adhere to not only the bylaws but also the association's canon of ethics. If you are looking for an agent, this is the place to start. They represent around 400 agents. There's a handy search tool, along with contact information to help you connect with agents.

Audiobook Publishing
Don't neglect audio when it comes to publishing your book. A lot of people don't have the time to sit down and read books. As they commute, work, or travel, they prefer to listen to audiobooks. In 2017, according to the Audio Publishers Association, total audiobook sales rose 22.7% to $2.1 billion and more than 50% of Americans have listened to an

audiobook. Those are impressive statistics and tell you why not to ignore audio. The audiobook market is growing very rapidly.

Getting your books in audio format should help grow your brand. For some Indie authors, audio has become a large chunk of their income. If you are getting ready to publish, consider having your book recorded into an audiobook. Reach out to an audio publisher and see if they are interested in your book.

If you are lucky, the publisher will bite and cover all recording and publishing costs. I've never paid a dime to have my audiobooks published, as the audio publishers were willing to compete to get my work into their audiobook libraries. That is the advantage of having a solid author platform when you market your books.

It is important to note, some authors prefer producing their own work. That usually means hiring a narrator or narrating the work themselves and then engaging an audio engineer to perform the recording.

I ultimately elected not to walk down this path. Why? Because I felt I did not need the headache of organizing or supervising the process, along with the time taken away from writing.

I feel it's important to note that I have personally worked with Audible Studios and Podium Publishing. Both companies have produced and published my books on audio and I seriously like what I've heard. They did bang-up jobs and I can't say enough about them.

I understand the other companies listed below provide excellent products too. Again, like anyone else you plan on working with, do your homework. Don't be afraid of speaking with them. There are some very nice and helpful people who work at these companies. Get to know them and their services. If you get a bite, awesome.

Ask them what they will do for marketing, and if you feel strongly about it, request a specific narrator you feel would be a good fit for your brand or for pre-approval of the narrator of their choice. The narrator can easily make or break an audiobook. Like popular authors, many narrators develop devoted followers.

The worst the audio publisher can tell you is, "No, you can't have that narrator." Remember, before you sell your rights, to carefully read over any agreement and consult a literary attorney.

ACX
Audible Studios
Author's Republic
AuthorDirect Audio
Blackstone Publishing
Brilliance Publishing
Findaway Voices
ListenUp Indie (IndiePub)
Podium Publishing
Oasis Audio
Tantor Media

Self-Publishing Platforms/Distributors

These are some of the publishing platforms available to you in the marketplace. This is where Indie authors go to publish and place their books for sale. It's also where readers go to find books to buy.

As I've said, Amazon is the 800-pound gorilla in the room and the primary focus of this book. I would recommend you seriously consider publishing with Amazon, especially if you want to make a splash and begin building brand. Across all platforms, Amazon sees the majority of eBook sales.

Publishing with Amazon increases the chances of building a successful author platform. That said, what works for me may not work for you. In the end, the choice is yours. It's your book and you are the one most qualified to make that very personal decision as to what platform to publish your book or books on. So, like everything else, educate yourself.

Learn about Amazon's competition and the differences between platforms. Then choose, making an informed decision.

Barnes & Noble Press
BookBaby
iBooks
IngramSpark
Kindle Direct Publishing (KDP)
Kobo
Lulu
Smashwords

Self-Publishing Services

These companies offer a range of services, like formatting or typesetting, to a complete publication solution. The prices for their services vary. I recommend you spend some time browsing through the list, visiting their websites, and reviewing services.

Pick several entities from my list or elsewhere and reach out. This is a great way to educate yourself and get to know the entity better. In addition to asking for recommendations, you can also perform a search to see if anyone's left online reviews.

Note: I engaged Telemachus Press to help me publish my first novel. They did a bang-up job. These days, Telemachus and 100 Covers provide me cover design services. I have never had a problem with Telemachus, and they've been super responsive to changes and are cost sensitive, which, in my world, is always a positive. The same goes for 100 Covers.

52 Novels
1106 Design
Author EMS
Author Help
BB eBooks
Bluewave Publishing
Blurb
BookBaby
Book Launchers
Book Reality
Bookouture
Bublish
Buzbooks
Clays
CompletelyNovel
Draft2Digital
Ebook Launch
eBook Partnership
FCM Publishing
Formatting Experts
Gatekeeper Press
Happy Self-Publishing
Independent Ink
IndieBookLauncher.com
Indie Publishing Group
MiblArt

MindStir
More Visual
Lulu
Luminare Press
Matador Publishing
Ocean Reeve Publishing
Outskirts Press
Page Publishing
PageMaster
Pixel Tweaks Publications
Prepare to Publish
SilverWood Books
Standout Books
Tablo
Telemachus Press
Whitefox
Woven Red Author Services

Cover Design

The companies below focus primarily on cover design. It is important to understand there is a difference between illustration and cover design. I hired my own illustrator, whom I found on Deviant Art https://www.deviantart.com/

My illustrator is a genius at bringing my vision to life. After I have the cover art, I then engage someone else to design a cover for me using the art. Some of the entities below provide both the illustration and cover design as a complete package.

I can't stress enough how important it is to have an awesome cover. If your cover does not grab a prospective reader's attention, people won't click through and you will lose sales. Note: For this book, I used 100 Covers for both illustration and cover design.

100 Covers
BEAUTeBOOk
Berge Design
Book Cover Express
Book Cover Service
Damonza
Dissect Designs
Ebooks Cover Design
Jessica Bell
JD Smith Design
Katie Birks
Robin Ludwig Design

Editorial Services

All books need editing. This includes developmental editing, copy editing, and proofreading. Do not neglect these steps. If you do, I am quite confident you will suffer poor reviews, which in turn will result in fewer sales.

Remember to find editors who work in the genre you are writing. Find someone you are comfortable working with and check their references. Also, you should check the reviews of books they've edited. Are they overwhelmingly positive or mediocre? That tells you a lot about not just the author but also the editor.

To help you better conduct your search, I am including several editorial associations and groups which have searchable lists of editors.

Editorial Freelancers Association
Northwest Editors Guild
The Society for Editing
National Association of Independent Writers and Editors
Reedsy

Author Tools—e Book Design and Writing Support
I made sure to include a few entities that provide tools, support, coaching, and other things I thought might prove helpful. Look them over. See if they are of use and benefit to you in growing your author platform.

Anthemion
Authority Authors
Author Accelerator
Author Marketing Club
BookFunnel
The Domino Project
Design for Writers
Kindlepreneur
Mark Dawson
Professional Writing Academy
ProWritingAid
Rethink Press
The Book Designer
Scribophile
Your Author Services
Writer's Digest
Writer's Market

Newsletter Service Providers
There are a good number of email marketing services out there from which to choose. I've listed a few reputable companies below. Again, if I sound like a broken record, there is a very good reason. I don't want you to get burned by the pan. Do your homework and find a company that is a good fit for your needs.

More importantly, choose one whose functions you can easily understand and use. YouTube should be a stop to determine the ease of use by watching a walkthrough of a particular service. Note: I use MailChimp and have had no serious issues with them, other than the occasional increase in price.

Benchmark
ConvertKit
MailChimp
Mailerlite

Book Marketing Sites

All of the sites listed here can help you market your book during promotions or book launches. I have personally used them. My preference is to utilize marketing services that have a newsletter feature, where the promotional deal ends up in the prospective reader's inbox. These types of marketing services seem to get the most bang for their buck, as opposed to just showing up on a website, posted to Facebook or on Twitter. I've starred the sites I've found particularly helpful in building my audience.

My recommendation would be to review each site, become familiar with how they market, and select the ones you feel are right for your needs. Not all advertising services are equal. Some promise the world and deliver very little.

As an Indie author, you have an opportunity to experiment with promotions and advertising to determine what works best for you.

When building a marketing plan around a book promotion or launch, I typically use several of the sites below in conjunction with social media advertising campaigns. A similar approach should help get you exposure to prospective readers and see additional purchases or downloads on your books, thereby growing your audience.

A few words of caution: Make certain your book is scheduled for KDP promotion before you begin booking the advertising. Sometimes people book the advertising, which can be tedious, but forget to set up the promotion.

Most of the marketing sites check to see if your book has been discounted or put up free on the day you indicated the promotion will start. If they find there is no KDP promotion running, the advertising does not run. It's a pain to go back and try to get refunds. Trust me on this; as unfortunately, I've had to do it.

Remember, building brand is a marathon, not a sprint. Every new reader helps you get closer to the finish line. With each promotion, you grow your reader base and grow your audience. These marketing sites should help you increase readership and sales.

Author Ad Network *
Author Cross-Promotion*
Author Marketing Club*
Awesome Gang
Bargain Booksy
Bargain EBook Hunters
Best Fantasy Books
Book Goodies
Book Kitty
BookLemur
Book of the Day
Book Reader Magazine
Book Bassett
Book Bongo
BookBub*
BookGorilla*
The Books Machine
BookHippo
Booksends
Book Tweeters

Booktastik
Choosy Bookworm
Daily Bookworm
Digital Book Today
Discount Book Man
eBookHounds*
eBookStage
eBooks Habit
eBookSoda
The eReader Café
Fire and Ice Book Tours
FK Books and Tips*
FreeBooksHub
FreeDiscountedBooks
The Fussy Librarian*
Genre Pulse
Goodkindles
Ignite Your Book
Indie Author News
Ink It
It's Write Now
JUST KINDLE BOOKS
Kindle Boards (KBoards)*
Kindle Book Promos
Kindle Mojo!
Kindle Nation Daily
Manybooks
My Book Cave
OHFB
Planet Books
ReadCheaply
Reading Deals
Robin Reads*

Additional Book Marketing Sites

I have not yet tried the following marketing sites but have heard good things about them. They are on my marketing bucket list. Check them out, and if you see solid results, please don't forget to let me know about your personal experience.

AllAuthor
Book Barbarian
BookBlast
bookdealio
BookDoggy
Books Go Social
Book Hub
Book Rebel
BookRunes
Booktalk
BookSweeps
Early Bird Books
eReaderIQ
Indie Book Lounge
LitRing
NewInBooks
The Portalist
Readers in the Know
Red Hot and Romantic
Red Roses Romance
Whizbuzz Books

Book Review Services

I am on the fence about a lot of these types of services. I've not yet run into an author who was completely satisfied with the results. What I mean by this is that they were not able to translate paid reviews into a significant amount of sales.

That does not mean you can't get these types of services to work for you. I could see them being particularly helpful when you first launch as an author. Get a few positive reviews and then build off that via online promotions coupled with the right amount of marketing and advertising.

On the other hand, if your book is good and you've engaged marketing outreach through advertising campaigns, readers should start to leave positive reviews on your books.

So, you could do both and hope to cash in, but I personally feel the money would be better spent on additional advertising and marketing campaigns. It all comes down to personal preference. In the end, the decision on how to proceed with your marketing and advertising plan is up to you. Be cautious. I've heard that Amazon and other platforms do not like any kind of paid reviews.

BlueInk Review
Kirkus
Online Book Club
Paid Author

Author Website Development

Below are a few web developers who exclusively focus on or have worked with authors. You should look for a web developer who is responsive and does good work.

By responsive, I mean that tasks are completed in a reasonable timeframe and changes should be made rapidly, preferably within hours. Ask for recommendations from current customers and review their work.

Note: I work with Axiom and have found them to be incredibly fast, responsive, and affordable. My agent introduced me to them.

Axiom
The Author Site
Author Website Central
Bakerview Consulting
Novel Website Design

Do It Yourself Web Development
Squarespace
WordPress
Wix
Weebly

Book Awards
If you don't enter contests, you can't win. But if you win, you can include your merits on your product page. Awards help convince new readers to try your work. This is brand building at its purest. It also feels nice to win and have your hard work recognized.

Some awards charge entrant fees. There is a lot of debate over such practices. You can easily do a search and read up on it. One such group that charges a fee is the IPPY's. I have won three IPPY awards myself and have found the recognition helpful in building and expanding my author platform.

More importantly, you can go to most bookstores and find IPPY-winning books on the shelves. However, you will have to do your homework and decide which contests are right for you to enter, fee or no fee.

Best Indie Book Award
Book of the Year Awards
Eric Hoffer
Golden Book Award

Goodreads Choice Book Awards
The Hugo Awards
IBPA Benjamin Franklin Awards
IndieBRAG
IPPY Awards
James River Writers Awards
Kindle Book Awards
Lamda Literary Awards (Lammy's)
Rubery Book Awards
The Wishing Shelf Book Awards
Writer's Digest
PNWA Writers Conference Contest

Important and Helpful Resources

Amazon Author Insights is a particularly great resource. There you will find articles that provide advice and tips designed to help the Indie author write, publish, and market their work. I have also included additional resources that I have found useful.

Amazon Author Insights
The Authors Guild
The Center for Fiction
Tips for how to use Goodreads

Facebook Group

I have established a Facebook Group: Every Writer's Dream: https://www.facebook.com/groups/1305583676263725/#

    This is a place for all types of writers and authors to come together to share, collaborate and connect. Basically, to discuss anything writing related. I envision this group as more of a support network and writing community than anything else.

MARC'S RULES

1. Do your research!
2. Make a business plan.
3. Plan ahead; think strategically.
4. Always use a professional.
5. Keep it simple, stupid!
6. If you think your idea for a book is cool, run with it. Don't listen to naysayers and don't solicit feedback.
7. No book is ever finished; it is only abandoned.
8. No one will care more about your work than you will.
9. Your book should be as polished as possible before you hand it off to your editor.
10. You need to be open to feedback.
11. Find an editor who has experience editing in your genre.
12. If you want the job done right, you are going to have to pay for it.
13. If I can do it, you can too!
14. Never begrudge a good agent their commission.
15. It is better to be educated than ignorant.
16. Keep the price affordable.
17. Become as organized as possible.
18. Create a comprehensive marketing and advertising plan.

Final Thoughts from the Author

It has become increasingly difficult for new Indie authors to stand out and achieve a measure of real success. I wrote this book to help aspiring authors have a better-than-average chance of succeeding in today's marketplace—in short, to give you an advantage. I hope you found this book useful, particularly the lists of services and resources. Remember to do your homework before engaging a company or service, including those I have listed above.

Being an author is certainly not easy. It is hard work—and I mean *hard* work—that takes dedication. At the same time, if writing is something you enjoy, being an author is fun. I truly enjoy my work, which means on most days it does not seem like work. That's important. If you're getting into writing to make bucket loads of money, you are doing it for the wrong reasons. Find something else to do...work that you enjoy and find rewarding. Life is too short to spend it toiling away at a job you dislike.

However, if being an author is truly your dream...I encourage you to follow it down the rabbit hole. Without making the attempt, you will never know if you could have been successful. So...take the first step, put yourself out there. Stumble along the way, make mistakes...if you fall down, that's okay. Life is about learning, gaining experience, and getting right back up on your feet. Pursue your dream to the fullest. Write, publish, and grow your brand, with the ultimate goal of building an author platform of your own.

If I can do it, so, too, can others.

Thank you for reading this book. If you are interested in learning more about my brand-building, one-on-one author mentoring or arranging a phone consultation, I would love to hear from you. Feel free to message me on Facebook or through my website, and please do not forget to leave a review on Amazon and Goodreads. Reviews keep me motivated and convince others to try my work.

I sincerely wish you all the success in the world,

Marc

Care to be notified when the next book is released and receive updates from the author?
Join the newsletter mailing list at Marc's website:

http://www.MAEnovels.com
Facebook: Marc Edelheit Author
Twitter: @MarcEdelheit

Made in the USA
Las Vegas, NV
08 November 2021